B&T 05/95 40.

W9-AKP-723

Presented through

The Haddonfield Friends

of The Library

SECRET GARDENS

REVEALED BY THEIR OWNERS

SECRET GARDENS

REVEALED BY THEIR OWNERS

Chosen and edited by

ROSEMARY VEREY
and
Katherine Lambert

A Bulfinch Press Book
Little, Brown and Company
Boston • New York • Toronto • London

PUBLIC LIBRARY
HADDONFIELD, NJ
08033

Text copyright © 1994 by Rosemary Verey
Illustrations by Simon Dorrell copyright © 1994 Ebury Press

All rights reserved. No part of this book may be reproduced in any
form or by any electronic or mechanical means, including information
storage and retrieval systems, without permission in writing from the
publisher, except by a reviewer who may quote brief passages in a
review.

First North American Edition
Second printing, 1994
Photograph copyright information appears on page 203.

ISBN 0-8212-2074-8

Library of Congress Catalog Card Number 93-86154

Bulfinch Press is an imprint and trademark of
Little, Brown and Company (Inc.)
Published simultaneously in Canada by
Little, Brown & Company (Canada) Limited

PRINTED IN ITALY

CONTENTS

167370

INTRODUCTION

Small Town Hideaways

In 1220, King Henry III instructed his bailiff at Woodstock 'to make round about the garden of our Queen two walls, good and high, so that no one may be able to enter, with a becoming and honourable herbary near our fish pond, in which the same Queen may be able to amuse herself.'

Seven centuries later, gardeners all over the world are still building 'good and high' walls, creating gardens within them, and, I hope, continuing to amuse themselves. This book speaks for all of them.

The essence of a secret garden is always elusive in that it relies as much on the imagination of the visitor as on the creator to make it a place of enchantment. Wandering along overgrown paths, strolling under trees, beside walls covered with climbers, distracted by pervading scents and the calls of hidden birds, it is a world enriched by thoughts of childhood and half-remembered moments in other gardens.

The secret garden is a recurring theme in history. It has never gone out of fashion. It may have changed in character over the world and over the centuries, but it restates itself in endless forms as a manifestation of one of man's most fundamental desires.

In Egypt, Persia and the Levant, gardens are defences against the tyrant of the region, the sun. In the oasis, walls or high banks protect the enclosure within from drying winds and the drifting sands of the desert. Only the vegetation which lies within reach of natural springs and irrigation can survive, and it is cultivated intensively on three levels: aloft, the date palms bear their life-sustaining fruit, the pomegranate and the apricot occupy the middle zone, while vegetables cover the soil between the irrigation channels.

Ornamental gardens of the Orient are refinements of this survival economy, with flowering trees and shrubs, parterres of herbs between rills of water, and the whole shaded by avenues of evergreens. Ch'angdokkung Palace in Seoul, started in 1405, has within its grounds a forest, and within the forest an eighteenth-century Biwon or secret garden where members of the court could go for peace and calm. In Kyoto, Japan you will find the Moss Temple, Saihoji, breath-taking in its beauty. Before the monks allow you to enter you must satisfy them by sitting, perhaps for an hour, contemplating, and at the scholar's table with brush and ink you must trace over the characters of an enormous sheet of prayers. At Katsuta you may request advance permission to enter the secret garden made in the seventeenth century for Prince Toshito as a hideaway and still owned today by the Imperial Household.

A panorama of images and descriptions of hidden, enclosed secret gardens flashes through my mind as I recall visits to Europe seeing gardens and galleries, and hours at home spent reading about early gardens – cloister and monastery, college and castle, Dutch gardens illustrated in 1583 by Vredeman De Vries, showing arbours and tunnels. In France in 1576 the engravings made by Jacques Androuet du Cerceau for Catherine de Medici reveal the 'inward' looking nature of the castle grounds always enclosed by high walls. Although the illustra-

Gardens Within Gardens

tions are architectural, the text reiterates that the windows have 'leur regard sur le jardin', also that the gardens are 'toutes fois fort beaux et bien entretenus'.

The beautifully illuminated page from a late fifteenth-century manuscript of the *Roman de la Rose* shows the lover outside the wall; after he has been admitted through the heavy wooden gate he approaches his lady in her private, secret garden. Less romantic but functional and enclosed is the castle courtyard garden illustrated in 1460 and previously described in the fourteenth century by the Italian, Piero de Crescenzi.

In its medieval form, the *giardino segreto* had been a *hortus conclusus* with a fountain, arbours and walls lined with turf seats, but in sophisticated Renaissance gardens it became transformed into a private enclosure for pleasure and intimate entertainment, in the process losing its religious symbolism and association with the Virgin Mary. The mid-fifteenth-century hanging garden of the Palazzo Piccolomini in Pienza has a spectacular view seen through the 'windows' of its surrounding walls and looking across the Val d'Orcia. The simplicity of its style gives it a haunting atmosphere as though the spirit of its creator, Pope Pius II, lives on. The 1572 Villa Capponi, hidden behind a high wall, has a true *giardino segreto* sheltered from the wind by its own crenellated wall. Most spectacular is the sunken garden at Villa Torrigiano which you reach down a double flight of balustraded stairs, passing through a dark passageway and a grotto before you find yourself in this small but exciting secret garden.

English books of the sixteen and seventeenth centuries leave us in no doubt that contemporary gardens were still surrounded by walls and hedges, that they must be enclosed against marauding soldiers, wandering cattle and thieves. In *The Gardeners Labyrinth* by Thomas Hyll (Didymus Mountain) published in 1577 the pictures are explicit, almost diagrammatic, showing that the garden should be enclosed by well-trimmed hedges or a high wall and only entered through a heavy wooden gate.

A few years later William Lawson, the Yorkshire clergyman, wrote:

'All your labour . . . is lost unless you fence well. Fruits are so delightsome . . . fence well therefore. Take heed of a door or window of any other mans into your orchard, yea though it be nailed up, or the wall be high, for perhaps they will prove thieves. Stone walls are best, both for fencing and lasting, and shrowding of your young trees; but about this you must bestow much pains and more cost, to have them handsome, high and durable.'

In 1620 Francis Bacon's preference was for a square garden 'encompassed on all four sides with a stately arched hedge . . . to be raised upon a bank, not steep, but gently sloped, of some six feet, set all with flowers.' Within the 'great hedge' were to be 'little low hedges, round, like welts, with some pretty pyramids' and 'in the very middle, a fair mount with three

Formal Enclosures

ascents and alleys', and a fountain. I think he would have enjoyed Sonny Garcia's garden in San Francisco, with its three berms and oriental fountain.

The frontispiece of the eighteenth-century *Gentleman's Recreation* shows a rectangular garden enclosed by a house and high walls. The author, John Lawrence, was a clergyman in Northamptonshire who was a keen advocate and teacher of fruit culture. He had much the same advice as William Lawson, but his amusing footnote runs:

'At my first coming to my parish, I found some difficulty to preserve my Fruit from Robbers. Hereupon I resolved upon this stratagem; I ordered the Smith to make a large Iron Trap, with formidable teeth, so close one within another, which was to be called a Man-Trap. *This was hung up for several weeks at the Smith's Shop* in terrorem, *giving it out, that now there would be great danger, if any one should attempt to rob my garden. This, without setting the Trap, succeeded according to my Wish, and I have not been since robbed these twelve years.'*

With the coming of the landscape movement in England, you might have thought that the secret garden would have no place. But it survived, separated from the house; at Knole in Kent as a wilderness laid out with walks and bluebells, at Nuneham Courtenay in Oxfordshire as a flower garden. Charles Reed's walled garden, hidden within his English park in Virginia, is a twentieth-century version of this theme.

The Victorian era saw the return of gardens near the house, but carpet bedding with gaudy, regimented planting destroyed any feeling of privacy. This was set out by the trained head gardener, but Jane Loudon came to the rescue of the Victorian ladies, explaining and encouraging them to regard gardening as a creative and worthwhile pursuit.

An enduring legacy of the Victorians was the secret gardens they conjured up in the books they wrote for children. There are many earlier examples, of course, like *Sleeping Beauty*, where the unfortunate prince must hack his way through a thorny undergrowth of roses and briars before attaining his princess. But it is *Alice in Wonderland* and above all *The Secret Garden* that carry the most enduring images of what a secret garden should be. The worlds in these books have a common thread: they fire the imagination of the children and as they discover the magic of nature their lives are changed for ever.

The restorers or creators of today's secret gardens are, I believe, inspired by the same longings that drove Alice or Mary. Lindie Wilson is now the mistress of a garden created by the legendary gardener Elizabeth Lawrence of North Carolina. Others, among them Constance Kargère or David Wheeler and Simon Dorrell, have chosen to make their own secret gardens.

In the USA there are numerous secret, hidden gardens and among those I have especially enjoyed are many in New Orleans, Charleston, South Carolina and in Boston, Mass-

Exuberant Gardens

achusetts. In the brilliant collection of short stories *Music for Chameleons* Truman Capote describes not secret gardens but secret cities:

> *'Some cities like wrapped boxes under Christmas trees, conceal unexpected gifts. . . . New Orleans, or so it seems to me, is the most secretive . . . where the prevalence of steep walls, of obscuring foliage, of tall thick locked iron gates, of dark tunnels leading to overgrown gardens where mimosa and camellias contrast colours, and lazing lizards flick their forked tongues, race along palm fronds . . . where cousins are whispering together as they sit under a fig tree beside the softly spilling fountain that cools their hidden garden.'*

Some gardens in any part of the world are secret by nature, by circumstance. Most town gardens are secret – how can a roof garden like Victor Nelson's in New York City not be so? Others are secret by design, but instinctively their creators respect the *genius loci*, like Dan Overly, who has refrained from imposing an 'English solution' on his Mississippi acres which he calls a 'redneck Japanese water garden'. Often there is an echo of childhood, as with Laura Fisher, Beatrice Bowles and Reiner Herling. My friend Bob Breitling in Atlanta, Georgia has planted a group of *Trachycarpus fortunei* out in his woods, so he can look down on them from his high deck and remember distant days in the Alabama swampland.

Many of the gardens in this book belong to my friends or are those I have been taken to to enjoy the special atmosphere. A day I will always remember was when I was allowed to walk in the roof-top garden at the Rockefeller Center – a garden seen by thousands of eyes from the surrounding windows of the high-rise buildings but where the only footsteps allowed are those of the gardeners who tend the flowers. I have the same feeling about the garden designed by Russell Page for the Frick Museum in New York, seen only from the street or from the windows of the museum. In cities throughout the world there must be hundreds of tiny gardens bursting with plant gems, secret because of the character of their owners. Drive through the countryside and you will catch glimpses of front gardens: you may be sure that behind the cottages will be quiet, secluded places. There are gardens within gardens, like Sylvia's Garden at Newby Hall, and others hidden in valleys or perched high on mountainsides.

At the heart of the matter, what is it that endows a garden with the quality of secrecy? One day, years ago, as my husband and I stood outside the gate of the Botanic Garden in Padua – created in 1545 – waiting patiently for the bell to be answered (the notice said 'OPEN') to be admitted into that walled garden, I was overwhelmed by a feeling of expectation, knowing that here I would find plants (the four hundred and fifty-year-old vitex in particular) which I had read and dreamed about. I would also find peace and the old patterns that so imbued it with a deep sense of history. I

Natural Gardens

picked up a seed from the paulownia tree and I have its historic descendant at Barnsley. I wonder who is clanging the bell now, awaiting admission to this special secret garden.

We must never forget the lessons from the past and new secret gardens will always be created. Today Barbara Robinson's and Oscar de la Renta's gardens, both in Connecticut, are magic oases among hills and woodland where you may pause awhile and time stands still. These gardens, and others like them are sanctuaries for the owners as they escape from the demands and pounding bustle of modern life. I am forever making new discoveries – this is what life is all about and what makes it so exciting.

ROSEMARY VEREY

SMALL TOWN HIDEAWAYS

Oh! it really is a werry pretty garden,
And Chingford to the eastward could be seen;
Wiv a ladder and some glasses,
You could see to 'Ackney Marshes,
If it wasn't for the 'ouses in between.

Edgar Bateman: a chorus from *The Cockney's Garden*

I

A CHILD'S INHERITANCE

Below a flowering quince, a stone angel looks out among ferns.

My FIRST SEVEN YEARS, I lived in the secret garden I live in now. Tucked into the steep east slope of Russian Hill, gardens and brown-shingled cottages are hidden from the street ninety steps below. Passers-by see only the tree tops of eucalyptus, redwood, hawthorn, Irish yew and Norfolk Island pine.

In my childhood, atop the hill above our house and behind one of San Francisco's few cork oaks, reigned my white-haired grandfather. When not keeping watch on the bay through his binoculars, he might call down to a son-in-law to prune a wayward branch or to a daughter (my mother's sister lived next door) to send up the grandchildren to watch him eat breakfast. Still in nightclothes, my brother and I would scramble up a narrow cascade of stone steps through rhododendrons taller than ourselves, racing to arrive at my grandfather's house ahead of our cousins, eager to be chosen to stir cream into Baba's coffee. Without a hang for fairness or my fiery devotion, nine times out of ten my brother or a boy cousin would win the stir and I would stand by and watch.

Afterwards, I'd swing into the blue and pink morning on a rope hanging from the eucalyptus, or stockpile smooth brown horse chestnuts hiding in spiked pods for the inter-tribal war we waged behind grown-up backs, or claim a sunny hiding place where sweet grass

From the front steps, a mossy path curves under an arch of *Clematis montana* var. *rubens* to the west-facing back deck. Over the writing and dining area, screened by wooden walls, hang the delicate blossoms of a double white-flowering cherry, *Prunus* 'Snow Queen'. Foliage conceals these terraces, with espaliered *Rhododendron* 'Fragrantissimum' above, *Camellia sasanqua* 'Setsugekka' at ground level.

soothed the soul while jolting the tongue. Often my aunt would lead us on nature walks around the hill. 'Mother Nature creates everything and everyone for a special purpose,' she'd say. I wondered if Mother Nature was God's mother or wife, and if they got along.

My father referred to our compound as Harmony Hill in mock tribute to the operatic gripes of his Irish in-laws – being English himself, his family conducted its rare arguments through lawyers. He came from a long line of gardeners and spent most weekends planting sun and shade perennials, a precarious business requiring ladders and ropes on the back slope, while my mother pruned wisteria, camellias and rhodo-dendrons in her still legendarily fierce style, and my brother and I weeded grumpily when plucked from roaming. Perhaps that is why my father nicknamed me 'Prunella'.

When I was seven, we moved away. Paradise was lost. Although we had a new garden in the Berkeley hills, sunnier and more open, I longed for my secret garden with its shelter-ing trees and hiding places, views of the bay, humming-birds, white butterflies who always flew in twos, and the rituals of my grand-father's steep realm. Whenever we visited him, I would creep down the back hill to stare, homesick, at our secret garden.

Twenty-two years later, I moved back to San Francisco just as the

stylish bachelor who had rented the house from our family for years moved out to marry a stylish widow. Delirious with excitement, I moved into Harmony Hill. The garden was still secret, but ivy flooded over every single inch except for the trees, one pink rhododendron which my parents had planted, and a wildly fragrant pale lavender heliotrope.

My single-handed assault on the demon ivy took three years. This amazonian task was mightily opposed by my daughter and son, to whom ivy on the back slope made a world-class slide. Only the arrival of a tiny wild calico kitten, whose mother sought childcare, distracted them enough for me to finish the job. The children went on to adopt countless cats, countering my protests with reminders of how I'd spoiled their slide. (Butterfly, the calico kitten, ruled as Queen of Cats for twenty-two years.)

Our first planting was an edible garden in two old raised stone beds curving around a brick path under the south-facing diningroom windows. Lettuces, chives, parsley, potatoes, chard, arugula, wild strawberries and apples appeared and disappeared while I read about the perennials my father had loved. After carpenters had built wooden retaining walls on the bare back slope, the hillside was ready to be replanted. Being drawn to fragrance, soft colors and fine foliage, I went to garden designer Stephen Suzman for a list of woodland

Seen through a cascade of *Rosa* 'Cécile Brunner', a glimpse of the stairway to the garden, ninety steps above street level. In the shelter of the tallest redwood in San Francisco grows a profusion of plants chosen for their fragrance, soft colours or fine foliage, including lavender heliotrope, pink *Rosa eglanteria, Erysimum* 'Bowles' Mauve', grey *Artemisia* 'Powis Castle', and green tree ferns.

plants suited to our temperate climate. Little by little I've planted almost all of them. *Ceanothus* 'Julia Phelps', *Pieris japonica*, luculia, abelia, *Magnolia stellata* and rhododendrons – 'Elsie Frye', 'Madame Masson', the dwarf 'Elisabeth Hobbie', 'Alice Fitzwilliams', 'Seta', 'Fragrantissimum' among them – were the first hill dwellers planted under the *Pinus radiata* my father's mother had brought in a five-gallon can on my parents' fifth wedding anniversary. The pine now towers forty feet high and requires the 'cloud pruning' of tree shaper Ted Kipping to let through the wind and light. Three interesting smaller trees added from Stephen's list are *Clethra arborea* from Madeira, *Oxydendrum arboreum* with its temple-dancer hands and crimson autumn leaves, and *Chimonanthus praecox*, wintersweet.

In time, I learned to plant *en masse*, and now a wall of espaliered *Rhododendron* 'Fragrantissimum' crosses the entire second bank of the slope, while *Camellia sasanqua* 'Setsugeka', underplanted with pink violets, and baby's tears, stand along the base. *Daphne odora*, 'Pearl Meidiland' roses and a double-flowering white cherry, *Prunus* 'Snow Queen', use the bed between levels to stage their ballet. Compost from a fifteen-foot bin behind the kitchen feeds the soil and, as the children taught me, makes wondrous weird underworld music if you stop to listen.

Vegetable gardening in the sunny south beds gave way to bedding of *Salvia clevelandii*, santolina, *Geranium pratense* and creeping thyme around a flowering quince in one bed, with Japanese anemones, rock roses, baby's tears and the infamous prunella spreading below the apple tree. *Clematis montana* var. *rubens* arches over the path, while blue-violet Chinese wisteria climbs past the diningroom windows and onto a trellis, sprawling over the most secret part of the garden.

Between the back slope and the French doors along the rear of the house runs a redwood deck. At one end, in a gazebo woven with jasmine, a hexagonal hot tub is hidden. Sweet woodruff and pale pink astilbe scent the edges, while the old

Beyond the bare branches of an old apple tree – host to *Clematis* 'Nelly Moser' – a fraction of San Francisco's cityscape is revealed. At the foot of the front steps is a bed of delphiniums and ranunculus edged with *Geranium endressii* 'Wargrave Pink' beneath a white-flowering quince. This tranquil corner, known only to those who climb from the street, is a reflection of the countryside in the heart of the city.

lavender heliotrope trails down from above. At the other end of the deck, a trellis of jasmine overhangs a maple, more sasanquas, and a writing dining-table. An ancient hedge of *Cestrum aurantiacum* screens the area by day and creates a seraglio of scent by night.

My secret garden offers me, as it did in childhood, beauty, comfort and delight. It was the place where I first discovered the connection to a matrix of boundless wisdom and love. I try and share that discovery with the children of today by working with the Strybing Arboretum and other public gardens and schools to develop their knowledge and love of gardening. I believe that every child should have access to nature and to the green magic it holds.

BEATRICE BOWLES, SAN FRANCISCO, CALIFORNIA

II

GUARDIANS OF A GARDEN

A painterly composition – *Clematis* 'Bees' Jubilee' and delphinium.

IN SUMMER, ONLY the trumpets of morning glory on the front of the London house – 15 Lawrence Street in Chelsea – proclaim the presence of the secret garden created by Patricia Casson.

But once, when an American couple were admiring the tubs beside the front door, she invited the strangers through to see the garden; they were followed, to her surprise, by a group of twenty to thirty more, also engaged in exploring Old Chelsea. Patricia Casson was delighted – for her, the particular joy of her garden lay in sharing it. If ever a garden was one woman's creation it is this; since her tragic death on holiday her family are determined that it will continue to be shared.

The first two centuries of the garden's history are unknown. Originally the land was part of the grounds of the Lawrence family's manor house, this became Monmouth House, in part of which lived the Georgian novelist Tobias Smollett. Then, for the middle years of the eighteenth century, it was occupied by the Chelsea Porcelain Manufactory, producing there its Red Anchor and Gold Anchor wares until the business moved to Derby and the old factory was demolished. A terrace of small brick houses was built on the site in Lawrence Street, occupied by a series of Chelsea worthies. Latterly, No. 15 was owned by the neighbouring Roman Catholic church and remained unmodernized.

When John and Patricia Casson bought it in 1970 it was in need of complete renovation.

Its garden was as enticing as a prison yard. A dismal patch of mud and brick paths, 70 foot long and 16 foot wide, bounded mostly by Georgian walls and decorated by a single misshapen cherry tree. There, one day, was found what looked like a muddy fragment of white bone; it turned out to be half a porcelain knife-handle, made by the Manufactory around 1750. Soon afterwards, when a small extension was being built behind the house as part of a ground-floor flat for John Casson's mother, Dame Sybil Thorndike, more broken porcelain was found and the Victoria and Albert Museum alerted.

The builders' excavations were extended by the ceramics experts, and they unearthed scores of porcelain fragments which had been used as drainage rubble around the foundations of the house – an almost complete rose-water ewer, large pieces of decorative tureens, plates, cups, a miniature greyhound from a group of figures and 'kiln furniture' from the factory itself. Most of this went to the Museum but the Cassons kept a few pieces to display beside complete examples.

While the archaeologists dug, so too did the Cassons, fertilizing the cat-poisoned earth and planting daffodil bulbs as they did so. The spring of 1971 promised more than one glorious summer.

The intimacy of this town garden reinterprets cottage garden exuberance with a range and sophistication of planting that is almost tropical. The urns are filled with purple petunias, pink roses and red poppies from Giverny. Hydrangeas echo the purple theme, phlox, lilies and a frill of nicotiana and impatiens the pink. Touches of yellow come from tall dahlias, lilies and *Choisya Ternata* 'Sundance'.

A riotous wall of climbing roses – red 'Malaga', yellow 'Marigold' and pink 'Botany Bay' – and purple-flowered *Clematis* 'Perle d'Azur' provide a background rich enough even for ecclesiastically purple delphiniums. Penstemons and the yellow Floribunda rose 'Kim' occupy the middle ground, purple aurbrieta, *Spiraea japonica* 'Goldflame' and variegated mint hide any bare ground.

The origins of Patricia's plans for her garden were varied. One was early memories of well-ordered country house gardens in Gloucestershire, where her own family, the Chester-Masters, lived, but she also wanted a bright cottage garden, with a patch of grass and a lot of colour. Another was sub-tropical Australia, where she, her husband and their three children had spent many years. Then there were friends' gardens, for she loved being shown their treasures and often left with seeds or cuttings.

Once the cherry had gone, the dominating feature was the huge ailanthus 'Tree of Heaven' in the garden next door. This cast some shade but was pruned regularly so that, while keeping its elegant, towering shape, it let as much sunlight as possible through its branches.

The Cassons introduced touches of their own: a bronze bust of Dame Sybil by Epstein was set on an ivy-covered plinth half-way down the garden on the south side. On the north side they sank a small pond with a little Florentine fountain, surrounded by a rock garden with stones brought from Scotland and France and huge flints from the Norfolk coast. The pond they populated with toads – the original pair came from the pet shop at Seven Dials where Charles Dickens had bought tortoises for his children – and with goldfish (later devoured by a heron).

Patricia chose a dozen varieties of camellia, such as she had come to love in Australia – 'Gloire de Nantes' is usually flowering by Christmas, augmented in summer with many different clematis. To these she added plants she had been given, and wildflowers grown from seed from Australia and Canada, where a son and daughter live. A huge and beautiful pink hollyhock grew year after year where the cherry tree had once stood. *Fremontodendron* 'California Glory' soared up the back of the house and many more plants contributed their striking looks and character. Each complemented its neighbour: *Choisya ternata* 'Sundance' showed to perfection against variegated leaves and the dark foliage of camellias.

This topography was drastically altered by the hurricane of 1987, when the Tree of Heaven crashed across the garden, knocking Dame Sybil off her plinth. Once the tree had been cut up and removed – and Dame Sybil presented to the National Portrait Gallery – sunlight was unimpeded and all things seemed possible in this garden for all seasons.

Patricia, who had once ridden in steeplechases and was a fine tennis player, was naturally competitive and could never resist entering competitions, although she affected to be embarrassed by the profusion of silver cups in her dining room. After being awarded the London Gardens Society's Certificate of Merit in 1972, two years after she had acquired the garden, she went on, over twenty years, to win innumerable prizes from the Chelsea Gardens Guild, Brighter Kensington and Chelsea, and various gardening societies. For the past five years the garden has been open under the National Gardens Scheme.

Despite her joy in sharing her secret garden, it has kept its intimacy. It was, and continues to be, a place for family meals in summer as an additional *al fresco* diningroom. Sometimes, when the bells of Chelsea Old Church peal and the surrounding houses shut out all noise of traffic on the Embankment, it is like a garden in a cathedral close. At night, dining by the light of flares, it can seem sub-tropical, scented by honeysuckles and a climbing 'Malaga' rose, with the toads lumbering along the brick paths to provide after-dinner entertainment.

John Casson, still at No. 15, and his daughter Penny – my wife – who lives with her family on the other side of the street, are carrying on Patricia's work according to her principles, but the garden, with its colour and exuberance, remains her own unique creation.

TOM POCOCK, CHELSEA, LONDON

III

THE SECRET GARDEN RECREATED

'The robin that befriended Mary and helped her to uncover the hidden entrance sits perched by the gate. Once inside, this is not the secret garden that Mary first saw . . . but the place of the book's ending, "a wilderness of . . . gold and purple and violet blue and flaming scarlet", a garden brought back to life, like the boy Colin himself, through the healing power of nature.'

O<small>N THE SMALL</small> island of Nantucket, the rain was coming down steadily. It was only the first week in September, but it was clearly not a day for the beach, and shopping in town, battling the elements, didn't seem appealing. Instead we decided to hire a good movie, light a warm fire and snuggle in for the afternoon. My husband Chuck and I and our two children loaded into the car for the quick sprint into town. None of us knew just how much impact this small event was to have.

Returning home with *The Secret Garden*, which I had loved reading as a child, the process was in play. The film began. Not too long into the plot, and much to the children's ire, we would rewind the tape, check out the walls, rewind, study the gates, rewind, look at the antique urns, rewind, get a feel of the apple tree, and then FLASH! Our next exhibit, for the March 1992 Philadelphia Flower Show, designed by Chuck and my father-in-law Charlie, would be The Secret Garden. The overall theme for the Show was to be 'Horizons for Discovery', and our idea certainly suited this.

Come now through the ivy-covered gate into Mary's discovery. The robin that befriended Mary and helped her to uncover the hidden entrance sits perched by the gate. Once inside, this is not the secret garden that Mary first saw, with the climbing roses as 'a mantle spreading over everything, walls, and trees, and even brown grass', but

The Secret Garden designed by the Gales for the 1992 Philadelphia Flower Show was inspired by the famous Victorian children's story, and aimed to recreate the excitement and wonder engendered by Mary's discovery of the garden behind the ivy-clad wall. Dickon's fox patrols the grass path leading to the garden pavilion, past a long pool set among rose hedges and a mass of country flowers.

the place of the book's ending, 'a wilderness of . . . gold and purple and violet blue and flaming scarlet', a garden brought back to life, like the boy Colin himself, through the healing power of nature.

The immediate focal point is a forty-foot pool filled with masses of water plants that leads the eye to a rose-covered stone pavilion. Next to the pool, a grass path allows you to venture down to this shady retreat, where Mary has used the bench as a post for her straw hat. Her garden tools are all around and many animal friends inhabit this space. The birds are tame and seem at peace as Mary moves amidst the profusion of plants. As you wander through the roses and perennials to the opposite side of the garden, you find another entrance to the fantasy, and looking back from this gate you see a large carved stone bench.

Should this garden remain a secret, known only to Mary and Dickon, Colin and his father, or should it be shared?

We took the liberty of sharing The Secret Garden with the crowds of people – 250,000 in all – who came to see the Philadelphia Flower Show that March.

Presenting our garden at a national indoor flower show was an exceptional challenge. The secret had to be viewed by thousands of dedicated gardeners, so a completely walled garden was out of the question. Our audience was expect-

ing to find an evocative recreation of the story they remembered from their childhood, wrapped up with other stories of secret rendezvous.

To tell the story of the children, the robin, the fox and the garden, we designed an amphitheatre-like exhibit with twelve-foot-high walls. The impression of a secret enclosure had to be convincing enough to attract visitors to the famous ivy-covered gate.

The mellow color of the masonry staging and the ivy-covered walls allowed for the mysterious feeling of the buried secret, the garden gate key. The walls cast shadows and hidden corners added to the intimation of secretive happenings. The final impact was the joy and love offered to the world by the earth through the beauty of her plants and flowers – the Magic, as Mary called it.

The construction of the garden was not so much magic as sheer hard work. We started with the pillars and the pavilion of antique-colored masonry Haddonstone. Four stone urns framed a vista to a focal point, a six-foot obelisk. The walls were matching stucco and flagstone capping. The ivy-covered gate evolved from a year of growth of English ivy on a wire structure filled with sphagnum moss.

Thirty-two-foot birch trees were forced and placed around

Breaching the borders of flowers that run alongside the forty-foot pool, two pairs of urns filled with geraniums signpost a cross-vista towards an obelisk framed by foxgloves, hollyhocks and delphiniums. The narrow bed in the foreground has nicotiana, delphiniums, ageratum and achillea; behind are the twin rose hedges. High walls, a thuja hedge and an arbour enclose the garden.

the outside of the walls to soften and conceal them, underplanted with leucothöe and lobelia. Forcing the plants for the show was a year-long project. Two growers and 12,000 square feet of greenhouse were required to produce the sixty-four varieties of plants for the original installation plus the replacements that were used while the show was in progress. We changed and groomed plants every evening after the show closed.

The perennials were two years old when they were put into coolers for a period of dormancy, or vernalization, in August. From the end of October to the middle of December, the perennials were placed in a cool house and gradually heated by altering the air and soil temperatures while the day length was increased by sodium vapor lighting.

The installation of the garden took thirty-three men nine days. The trip from our nursery to the Civic Center was sometimes a challenge, with frigid temperatures, blizzards and traffic jams adding to the excitement. But it was finally Show Time, and yes, we had a real winner! The Secret Garden brought us 98 points, four pieces of silver, a visit and photo session with the then First Lady Barbara Bush, and dozens of news media happenings. Hundreds of man hours had paid off.

BARBARA GALE, THE SECRET GARDEN AT THE PHILADELPHIA FLOWER SHOW, 1992

IV
TROPICAL TERRACES

'Lavender Dream' roses peer through pink and grey balustrading.

IN THE FALL of 1985 my partner Tom Valva and I purchased a home on the southern edge of San Francisco. The houses have only five feet of space between them, and our backyard is accessible on either side through these narrow alleys. For privacy and security, high wooden gates were installed at the end of each alley before you reach the back garden, which is hidden from the street. The small front garden gives only a hint that a secret garden can be discovered behind the house and that fanatical gardeners live here.

Our house is only about five miles from the Pacific Ocean, which explains why this area of San Francisco is windy, foggy and colder than most parts of the city, especially during the summer months. It was quite a misnomer to label this district 'Sunnyside' when it is just the opposite! These three climatic elements were crucial factors in the creation of our gardens.

It was not until the summer of 1986 that I started to plan and lay out the gardens. The small streetside front garden would be simple, low-maintenance and wind-tolerant, because the front of the house is constantly exposed to gusty winds. The back garden, more protected from the elements, would be designed with architectural and sculptural features and, of course, bountiful collections of rare and unusual plants.

With excitement, determination and ambition, we worked on the backyard garden first. The plot is only 30 by 60 feet and very flat. There was previously a lawn with a two-foot-wide concrete perimeter walkway. The only feature we preserved was a venerable old escallonia that had grown into a tree with a trunk two feet in diameter. Approximately 100 years old, it is now a beautiful backdrop behind a raised deck which has bcome the focal point of the new garden.

The construction of the architectural elements started with the lathhouse attached to the residence, which has doors opening into both house and garden. Half of the lathhouse is protected by the overhang of the second-floor sunroom. Here Tom and I created a tropical rainforest garden, complete with a pond and waterfall. With the soil dug out from the pond, we built a raised berm directly outside the lathhouse, and arranged rocks in a naturalistic way around the berm to hold the soil in place.

The existing lawn gave way to a central patio created with inexpensive gray concrete pavers – gray was chosen as the perfect background for the colorful plants of the future. At the back edge of the patio we built a barbecue grill with gray cobblestones, and behind it added a redwood deck raised eight inches from the ground.

To the far right is a redwood pergola which will in time be cascading with glorious vines. Beneath the pergola is another raised area with a gently flowing fountain fashioned from a wonderful oriental urn with cascades of copper ivy. To add more drama, a tall mirror was positioned to reflect light and to give more depth to this shady space; your eye is tricked into believing that there is a *double* oriental urn fountain in front of it. A sparrow soon discovered the mirror and, fascinated, danced in front of it for several days.

The last structure to be built was another redwood deck, the focal point of the garden. This deck appears at first to be the center stage, but it is merely the vantage point for the viewer – the performers are the plants that surround it. As you step up onto the deck, you will notice a myriad of potted plants which adorn every possible space.

Approximately one-third of the plants in the garden are in containers, which gives flexibility as they can be easily rearranged and moved so you can display a plant in season or hide it away when its beauty has faded.

There are five different levels in all, including a balcony on the second floor of the house overlooking the garden. Common belief is that different levels in a small space look 'chopped-up' and smaller. On the contrary, small gardens can look bigger if the elevated spaces gradually flow from one level to another: more surface area is created and consequently the plants display better. As you step up onto the first level, stop for a moment and look at the garden from this angle. Your eye is led to believe that the garden is bigger than it actually is, since it is difficult to determine exactly where the garden ends.

The small size of the lot did not discourage me from doing all the things I have always wanted to do. Being an architect by profession, it was not difficult for me to visualize what I

Looking from the elevated deck back towards the house, with its characterful Victorian detailing. Although the garden is only 30 by 60 feet, the density and verticality of the planting create an illusion of infinite space, and the rich colour scheme and eclectic choice of plants give a tropical feel. The stone barbecue grill adds structure and also serves as a part-time 'propagating pit'.

wanted the garden to become. It would have different rooms on various levels and include mounds supported by rocks to break the flatness of the ground and increase the surface area for plants. There would have to be water, for its tranquil and soothing sound masks urban noise and comforts the soul. The plant materials would be lush, almost tropical, to remind me of my childhood in the Philippines. But most of all, no matter how small the garden, it would be mysterious and sensual and not be seen all at once. The eye would be allowed to wander and explore and gradually discover what was behind every façade of greenery.

Once all the architectural elements in the garden were completed, came the most exciting aspect of creating a garden: the process of plant selection. Since San Francisco is blessed with very mild winters, an enormous palette of plants is available. The look of a tropical garden can be achieved easily by using many sub-tropical plants that thrive in the Bay Area. Foliage chosen for color, form and texture – especially bold and variegated varieties – plays a major role which allows the show to go on all year round. Although the entire garden is fenced, the property line is masked by the dense assemblage of flora, its verticality giving the illusion of infinity. As your eyes wander, the intricate and unusual juxtaposition of colors, textures and forms becomes evident.

PREVIOUS PAGE: Beneath the pergola is a shady spot
brightened by mounds of yellow-variegated carex,
golden-leaved *Acorus gramineus* 'Ogon', *Houttuynia cordata* 'Chameleon' and red-foliaged *Begonia grandis*. A
tall mirror against the fence reflects light and creates
an illusion of depth, tricking your eyes into believing
there is a *double* urn fountain in front of it.

The problems of wind, fog and a cooler climate have their merits and this garden takes full advantage of them. The density of the plantings requires plenty of air movement and circulation to minimize insect, fungus and mildew infestation; but because the plants are spaced closely, they tend to support each other from the strong wind; and the fog keeps the garden moist, reducing the frequency of watering. This is also one reason for the inclusion of many plants that grow in the cloud forests of Mexico. And since this area is much cooler than most parts of the Bay Area, the foliage is lusher and the blooming season extends longer. My preference for bright warm colors in lieu of 'safe pastels' has a lot to do with the often foggy and dreary days that linger in the summer months. Vibrant yellows, reds, pinks, purples, oranges and bronzes brighten up the garden and give a warmer feeling.

The very center of the garden was kept open to create an illusion of a bigger space, and to give breath from the surrounding landscape. The sheer density and intracacy of the plantings can be overwhelming, especially to the novice visitor. If you turn to face the back of the house you are confronted with the most complex plant and color combinations in the garden. This raised area in front of the lathhouse, ornamented with Victorian embellishments, recalls the tropical theme within, with vines, shrubs and perennials creating a tapestry of color interwoven with herbaceous plants.

One of my favorite plant combinations in the garden is to be found along one of the paths leading to the central space. The arching green and yellow blades of *Cortaderia selloana* 'Sunstripe' weave intricately around the reddish chocolate-brown broad straps of *Phormium* 'Dark Delight'; close by is a bonsaied *Fagus sylvatica* 'Purpurea Pendula' with a tall background of *Fuchsia excorticata* var. *purpurescens*, its purple leaves becoming more beautiful as it sways in the breeze, showing off its silvery underside.

There are many unusual plants in the garden, selected from speciality nurseries all over the country. Among them are two cannas, *Canna* 'Cleopatra', with irregular purple swirls on its leaves, and the very rare *C.* 'Durban', undoubtedly possessing the most colorful foliage in the plant kingdom, with various shades of orange, red, yellow, green, purple and rose splashed all over the entire leaf surface. There is also a rare *Gunnera insignis* with red stalks, red-veined foliage and an unusual spray of pink flowers. Most garden books will tell you not to use anything that is big in a small garden. I don't agree!

The best spot to have an overview of our small paradise is from the stairs leading to the elevated deck. Cascading out of the Victorian railings is the luxurious growth of a variegated form of *Helichrysum petiolare* combined with the silvery-white foliage of *Calocephalus brownii*. Glorious vines leap for the best position on this center stage. Not to be outshone are the pendulous scarlet flowers of the ever-blooming *Fuchsia* 'Fanfare'. In the background, our beloved century-old escallonia tree, its gnarled branches bursting with colorful bromeliads, stands patiently as a sentinel to this ever-changing garden.

As I look out from above, I see the pendulous wands of the dierama swaying gracefully in the breeze, and hear the song of the birds and the merry buzzing of the bees. Tom and I are honored for our garden to be in the pages of this book and in the company of these beautiful secret gardens. But sometimes I wonder if the humming-birds, the sparrows, the mockingbirds, the butterflies and the bees will approve, since our secret garden will not be so secret any more!

SONNY GARCIA, SAN FRANCISCO, CALIFORNIA

V

ORDER AND EXUBERANCE

Pure white foxgloves mingle with white daisies.

SPREAD OUT CLOSE to the beach and water along the English Channel on the French coast between Dieppe and St Valéry are a number of small villages. One of these, however, Varengeville-sur-Mer, stands high on the cliffs; from the twelfth-century church and its marine churchyard a spectacular view opens up. Here Saint Valéry obeyed a voice telling him to build a sanctuary – not in the middle of the village but on the very edge of the cliff. All legends convey a sense of magic, and this one may have inspired other people to use old stones for building, so that Varengeville today is a privileged site with its cottages, old farmhouses, historic manors and, of course, gardens. Some of these gardens are open to view, while others are hidden from the road by high hedgerows, so that one can only guess at what lies behind them.

One of these small gardens is more secret than the rest. Hidden behind a hawthorn hedge, next to an apple orchard, it ambles from a white clapboard house in an organized design of natural disorder. Climbing roses rising above the apple trees, clematis intertwined amongst bushes and garlands of roses losing themselves along a wooden pergola, give only the slightest clue to what has been carefully disposed in a series of rooms, surprising the visitor unfamiliar with the design. The entrances to each room are either yew door frames or small white portals. Much of the

atmosphere can be related to Kate Greenaway and other English illustrators who coloured my childhood.

The secrecy was by no means intentional. Some twenty years ago a few stray cows wandered through the half-closed gate leading from the orchard and stared at my mother-in-law through her window panes as she was having tea, but not before they had trampled all over the lawns and nibbled at the roses which were my first attempt at creating a garden. I was given permission to transform part of the orchard into a garden of my own, but only square by square, room by room.

To give both protection from high winds and some privacy, yew hedges became the walls. They gave a sense of enclosure and enabled me to arrange and design the borders, plant box, holly and hawthorn, and introduce flowers, which today have multiplied to the point where I spend most of my time trying to fit in one more and being thankful for any bare space.

At the outset the hedges were low, and I used to resent any intrusion from grown-ups; only children, being small, seemed to fit in naturally. Ruskin said that 'a garden should be dark and wild' – difficult to achieve when nothing has had time to grow to any size. Today his remark is more apposite: the seasons have permitted nature to dictate its shapes and obvious inclinations; simple tresses of roses have become tangles of colour, intermingled with the

OVERLEAF: A fairytale glimpse through an archway cut into one of the yew walls surrounding the garden reveals a mushroom of clipped standard box with purple sage at its feet. At the head of the arch, pink flowers stray into purple territory as *Rosa* 'Constance Spry' meets *Clematis* 'Nelly Moser', underplanted with *Geranium pratense* and white foxgloves. Here romance and formality go hand in hand.

delicate and subtle tones of clematis.

'A garden is a metaphysical creation,' said Lawrence Johnston, the maker of Hidcote, 'but is it the metaphysics which create the garden or the garden which creates the metaphysics?' Put more simply, a garden reflects the character of its creator. In my eyes secrecy is a personal attribute which comes from within and can only be transformed into shapes and colours after many years' study of gardening books and lots of visits to see other people's gardens.

Secrecy implies a charm of its own – something secret is something intimate, personal. This is what I am trying to

ABOVE: In June, roses, clematis and poppies, lilies, alliums and Miss Wilmott's ghost bloom with exuberance in this, the heart of the garden. Four clipped box balls mount guard on the tiny reflecting pool.
RIGHT: Wooden tubs of *Viburnum carlesii* signal the entrance to the orchard. White foxgloves are silhouetted against the dark-green yew foliage, and *Rosa* 'Seagull' hovers above the gate.

create in the garden. I sometimes fall in love with some arrangement of colour and structure: a well-balanced order amidst natural exuberance.

Enjoying the song thrushes, blackbirds and pigeons splashing in square brick bird baths, walking along an *allée* of asters and causing a flurry of butterflies at each step, smelling a profusion of wonderful scents all over the garden, watching the stream of light and the shadows – all of these impressions are silent, thus secret, and most of all give pleasure to the one who spends all year working on her knees striving to make this vision her reality.

CONSTANCE KARGERE, VARENGEVILLE-SUR-MER, FRANCE

VI

A STUDY IN GREEN

Potted plants set among laurel and pebbles from Chesil Beach.

I WAS BROUGHT UP in the country, where I was used to a large garden with plenty of space to give me the freedom of escape. Not only were there secret retreats away from tiresome adults, but different parts of the garden suited different moods, and each part led into its own private world. The ordered refinement of the rose garden, the sensual promise of fruit in the kitchen garden, the brooding melancholy of the fir trees, all these made a kaleidoscope to which my childish imagination could respond.

Several years and a few gardens later, I moved to a small town house in Dorchester. I had only to look from a first-floor window at other gardens in the same terrace to realize the limitations of my cramped sixteen-foot-wide plot. There were few secret corners and few surprises. Untended for years, it consisted largely of an incredibly lusty patch of brambles some reaching over seven feet tall. I now realize that it was the singularity of their wild profusion that gave me the confidence to let plants grow as they have, dictating their occupancy of this tiny space.

I have tried to distil some of the richness I remember from

A curtain of foliage, rich in shape and texture, keeps the garden completely concealed. Deep-green Italian cypress and lustrous *Pittosporum tobira* form the backdrop, while the sword-shaped leaves and pale flower columns of *Sisyrinchium striatum* echo the form of the stone cherub standing among *Convolvulus cneorum*, with *Juniperus squamata* 'Blue Carpet' spreading to cover the ground at his feet.

my childhood garden by the use of contrast – vital if interest is to be retained. As this is not a garden packed full with flowering plants I have tried to conjure up drama and variety by juxtaposing different shapes and textures of foliage – the solid mass of a bay tree next to the sketchiness of variegated dogwood, the slender darkness of cypress with the spreading lightness of a grey pear.

For added interest I tried planting miniature cyclamen under the pear tree, but marauding cats use it as a climbing frame, so I have given up the unequal struggle; a circle of gravel, edged with tiles, provides a difference of shape that is acceptable compensation. The chequerboard effect near the house includes pebbles from Chesil Beach (scooped up when their removal was still allowed). The sound they make when walked upon is very satisfying and they contrast with what I like to imagine is smooth green grass.

The bushes have now grown up and filled out, helping to create the illusion of a garden containing more worlds than it really does, especially as you cannot see all of it at once. At times the gardens on each side seem, not feet, but miles away.

ANTHONY KILROY, DORCHESTER, DORSET

VII

HIGH-WALLED HAVEN

'When we returned to our native Charleston after many years, the fourteen-foot brick walls and long narrow-necked driveway of this hidden garden intrigued us.'

I N CHARLESTON we have a saying: 'Tall walls do good neighbors make.' The high walls of our courtyard garden certainly make excellent neighbors, but when the gate is open wide visitors are always welcome.

Bedon Alley connects Elliott and Tradd Streets, two of the oldest in Charleston. Anyone walking along it encounters brick walls mounted with assorted cannon balls, gargoyles and wrought-iron fencing; large banana leaves glisten and beckon in the wind. Close to the harbor, the narrow alley once provided rear access to a dairy, a carriage yard, a mill and a cotton warehouse. Ghosts seem to walk the street during candlelit tours of the area.

When we returned to our native Charleston after many years, the fourteen-foot brick walls and long narrow-necked driveway of this hidden garden intrigued us. The private world within offered my late wife Betty a peaceful retreat after a period of chemotherapy to treat bone cancer. By her training as a surgical nurse and her skill and inclination as an artist, we felt that the garden would become a serene haven where together we could watch the birds and wildlife. My role was to be the hired hand, who under her tutelage maintained the grounds and steadily improved the planting season by season.

Guided by our trusted landscape architects, Hugh and Mary Palmer Dargan, the first challenge in this small space was to soften the straight lines by creating eye-catching curves. The focal point of the garden is now a fountain with La Brezza dancing in the gentle spray of twin water-lilies; its bluestone ledge is a perfect place for grandchildren to sit and feed the goldfish. Pennsylvania bluestone is used both here and under the arbor to enhance the feeling of space, flowing seamlessly into the grass panel. Accentuating the fountain are terracotta pots filled with a number of colorful seasonal plantings of petunias, geraniums, pansies or alyssum.

In the backdrop behind the fountain loomed a neighboring house with three windows peering into our very private space, so we transplanted *Photinia serrulata* at least eighteen feet tall to obscure the offending apertures. On the other wall, flanking the front path, we encouraged *Rosa banksiae* and *Vitex agnus-castus* to make a long green tunnel, with mossy English brick paving leading to the front door. This path looks and feels old, overgrown and mysterious.

Intertwining across the old brick walls are splendid vines – mandevilla species and the Confederate jasmine, *Trachelospermum floridanum*. Flowering ginger and maidenhair fern dominate the plantings at the base of the wall, associating well with the evergreen *Aspidistra elatior*; in the late spring they receive infusions of impatiens.

Flanking the two entrances into the garden, four trios of *Buxus micro-*

Entering the garden from the street, your eye is caught by La Brezza dancing in the fountain, with pink mandevilla vine looping around her to meet the pink impatiens in terracotta pots at her feet. As you reach the arbour at the other end, you turn to see that she is the garden's focal point. Mellow brick and bluestone-capped wall and paving create an atmosphere of settled maturity.

phylla var. *japonica* make their clipped and balanced statement. The grass lozenge in the central corridor is a carpet of the local 'Charleston grass', tough enough to withstand intermittent sunlight and even the rompings of Muffin, our elderly shitzu.

The north part of the garden is shaded by the mature photinias and the fourteen-foot wall. Here a cut-leaf *Acer palmatum* 'Bloodgood' provides textural interest and vivid red foliage, and on the northern fringe of the garden the blue lacecap hydrangea introduces its wonderful variegated foliage and blue flowers in midsummer to enliven the shady setting.

The south side is sunny; there are fewer trees and a lower wall, with ivy cascading over from the neighbor's side. We

From the arbour, also paved with bluestone, stretch matching serpentine brick-edged beds filled with low plants. The walls are a backcloth for high planting – cut-leaf maples against the fourteen-foot wall of the old dairy on the right, photinias screening out the neighbours at the far end. The kitchen garden bed bordering the path on the left has standard tea roses amongst the herbs.

both loved to cook, so a kitchen garden was incorporated into the border, where standard tea roses are successfully underplanted with prostrate rosemary, lemon balm, mint, parsley and oregano. An occasional miniature tomato plant is encouraged to join this amiable *mélange*.

The arbor next to the house is part and parcel of our secret garden. Providing shade for the rooms inside the house and floral color at different times of the year, the enclosure of arbor and vines makes it a private room within the garden itself. Betty designed the twig-style garden furniture herself and it was built to her specifications by Rick Avrett of Olde Charleston Forge. Like every detail in this diminutive garden, it is a personal statement.

LOUIE KOESTER, CHARLESTON, SOUTH CAROLINA

VIII

UNDER THE CHURCH TOWER

> *F*rom the house you step into a
> walled, triangular, brick-paved terrace
> . . . A corner leads into a corridor paved
> with irregular pieces of Hornton stone
> and at the end of this shady passage a
> sunlit opening invites you to step onto the
> terrace beside the pool. The element of
> surprise at this point continues to
> enchant me.'

MEDIEVAL WARWICK was laid out with security in mind. The houses in the four principal streets were built shoulder to shoulder to form an unbroken wall, accessible only from individual front doors and carriage gates. In 1694 a widespread fire destroyed the medieval heart of the city, but in the Georgian-style rebuilding the layout was repeated. The area enclosed is a jigsaw puzzle of interlocking spaces, some now opened to car parking, but still with sufficient gardens and large trees to maintain the illusion of a tranquil oasis within the centre of a bustling town.

I examined 13 Church Street with a view to purchase in 1959. It provided an office as well as living accommodation, both of which I needed in order to start a landscape design practice and raise a family. The garden was rather small and separated from the house by a walled corridor, but this feature intrigued me, and the presence of a seventy-foot walnut tree enveloping it was quite awe-inspiring. Local enquiries revealed that an adjoining garden, completely overgrown with brambles and sycamores, was also available. Discovering this, I hesitated no longer, and succeeded in buying the property.

Having moved in, the first essential was to provide a playing surface for the children, so with their help we cleared the overgrown garden and made a lawn. The treatment of the ten-foot-high wall dividing the

OVERLEAF: Terracotta pots filled with flowers or clipped box balls flank the path leading to the pool garden, where a mellow brick arch frames the lead figure of a classical water-carrier. Above low hedges and amidst green foliage, accents of white, pink, fuchsia and brilliant red reach an eye-catching height in the distinctive copper leaves and scarlet flowers of *Dahlia* 'Bishop of Llandaff'.

gardens was our most important design decision. Should we take it away to make a single space, or reduce its height and create openings through it? The latter provided the more interesting opportunities and, although the garden has developed considerably since then, this is the one feature which has remained unchanged and has determined the subsequent layout.

From the house you step into a walled, triangular, brick-paved terrace, laid originally underneath a walnut tree, which alas is no longer with us. A corner leads into a corridor paved with irregular pieces of Hornton stone and at the end of this shady passage a sunlit opening invites you to step onto the terrace beside the pool. The element of surprise at this point continues to enchant me. Two paces on is yet another surprise: a wall arch on the left reveals the existence of a further garden. A footpath leads through the arch and, veering to the right, joins a short flight of sandstone steps which rise to the paving on the far side of the pool, so completing a circuit.

The need for a playing space soon proved illusory. The more active ball games were quite impractical, and in any case daughters outnumbered sons and followed less space-demanding pursuits. I began to think of more interesting ways of developing the layout.

With the exception of the splendid tower of St Mary's Church, the view from the garden of roof tops and

backs of houses, while full of character, was nevertheless a distraction, especially on the south and east boundaries where the walls do not exceed six feet. I decided to increase the sense of enclosure by constructing detached brick piers in front of the walls to support pergola rails which could be draped in vegetation. This was at its most successful when *Vitis coignetiae*, which holds all other climbers in derision, took absolute charge.

The pool owes its genesis to a flight of fancy which was never achieved – that of mirroring the church tower in its surface. This would have been a *tour de force* if my calculations had not somewhere been at fault. On nights when the corona of the tower is floodlit there is a corresponding glow in the water, and I comfort myself that I almost succeeded. Reflection apart, the pool is the dominant feature. It is central and deliberately formal, crossed by stepping stones and embraced by luxuriant planting, which springs not only from the sides but also from the wall tops and pergola above.

Beyond the pool tall planting tempers the appearance of a windowless two-storey building rendered with rough-cast stucco. A combination of tall evergreen shrubs with relatively light deciduous trees has achieved the desired effect. The two

ABOVE: In the water garden a primitive Portland stone head carved by Lucy Smith stands out against dark shadows, framed in August by purple clematis and *Brachyglottis greyi*. RIGHT: Pebbles contained in a semi-circle, kept moist by a lizard fountain by the same artist, play host to ajuga, lysimachia, saxifrage and hosta, with *Fuchsia* 'Thalia' in a pot nearby.

gardens join at this point but are seen in sequence rather than together and provide different experiences. In contrast to the water garden the outlines are flowing and serpentine, the dominant feature a 'pool' of close-mown grass contained by a low curving dam of brickwork.

In both gardens the general planting is formed with a ground layer of low herbaceous plants punctuated informally by taller perennials, shrubs and trees. Included in this is a community of self-sown plants – Welsh poppies, Spanish bluebells, violets, aquilegias, foxgloves, forget-me-nots and honesty. These contribute a spontaneous quality, in sharp contrast to the borders edged with clipped box, which in spring are planted with dark red wallflowers and white tulips, whilst yellow or pink tulips are paired with myosotis in the adjoining earthenware pots.

Winter is a serious test of a garden's visual character and provides the designer with an interesting challenge. Whilst I look forward with excitement to the opening of the incredible buds of the tree peonies, to the rich scent of 'Constance Spry' roses, the strongest impulse of all is to renew my annual acquaintance with the snowdrop. Not a single one, of course – I dream of them in masses.

GEOFFREY SMITH, WARWICK, WARWICKSHIRE

IX

A RAIN FOREST IN THE CITY

A variegated canna blooms among the golden foliage of robinia.

In the heart of a high-rise city it is still possible to find secret gardens of beauty, peace and serenity, soothing the senses with their textures, sounds and fragrance. Over the years my own garden in Manhattan has become a small rain forest, asserting itself above the noise and frenzy of New York. Amongst the thousands of plants a wall fountain plays gently and hanging chimes swing in the soft breezes, creating their own background music. A path winds through the garden with its wealth of hidden treasures.

Over 200 containers fill my 30-foot by 15-foot city space on top of a two-floor extension to my brownstone house, which is over 100 years old. Flowers leap out at you from every level, and because the many containers are raised, one sees the plants from the perspective of a child lying on the ground. In my garden the eye is directed upward as well as outward: I've placed several twelve-foot birch trunk to give the illusion of a garden reaching towards the sky. These trunks provide support for my wide collection of vines, and their colored bark makes a pleasing contrast with the many shades of green.

By using every inch of the limited space it is possible to create a full, rich and varied garden of many plants with only a few of each cultivar. My plant collection is eclectic. It includes

Mounting the steps into this plant-filled roof garden is a horticultural experience. You are immediately surrounded by flowers at all levels, brimming from over two hundred containers. Climbers entwine wherever they can. A Norway maple provides shade for plants and people on hot summer days; by evening, the garden is lit with twinkle lights and filled with scent and the sound of music.

fully grown hostas ranging from three inches to three feet; day lilies and hybrid lilies which do well in shade; vines such as clematis; several kinds of honeysuckle and an amphalopsis trumpet vine; many maple trees which automatically become bonsaied because of the size of the pots; while a multitude of variegated plants bring light and shadow into the garden, and several plants with chartreuse foliage create points of light. My collection of house plants thrives outdoors in the summer and adds a tropical touch.

Since I do not use many annuals, each container has several different types of flowering plant so that there is continuous color throughout the season. Because of my desire for a wide variety I often challenge and stretch the given limits for light and temperature. Since this is a container garden I am able to reposition the plants to match my changing sense of design and to display the plants as they naturally grow.

Being a shade garden, it is a comfortable retreat from the day's strong light, the perfect place to read, eat or relax. However, the evening is my favorite time on the terrace, the time when, sitting under the small twinkle light concealed in the six-storey high Norway maple which acts as an umbrella over the table, I most often share the garden with friends.

Victor Nelson, New York City

X
AT THE TOP OF THE STAIRS

A pale, distinctive trio of eryngium, lilies and astrantia.

Push open the wrought-iron gate leading off the steep little street on a summer's afternoon, and you are immediately in the Mediterranean – on a south-facing terrace filled with fragrant plants in pots, and the front door overhung with clematis and roses. Then you notice a wooden staircase against the wall, covered with *Wisteria sinensis*, leading upwards, apparently nowhere, like a flight of outsize library steps. You simply must climb them, and yes, there is a gate in the wall at the top, completely screened by the wisteria. Perhaps a gust of wind will reveal the entrance to you, as it did to Mary Lennox in the most famous secret garden of them all.

You must step carefully over the gnarled grey tree roots, laid obligingly flat as a sill, and you are in my own secret garden. It is high above the street, but straight ahead the land rises higher, up to the old windmill, stripped now of its sails but towering still, a friendly guardian, above the garden. Down to the right the land slopes to meet the mellow roofscape of rust-coloured Roman pantiles on my neighbours' houses, and in the distance is the glint of the River Deben. In between there are lawns and borders, flowing and winding like the river itself. The air is completely still, quiet but for the small sounds of birds; soon the light will deepen and the moon begin to highlight the silver foliage, throwing dark shadows onto the sloping lawn.

At the top of the staircase, a curtain of wisteria parts to reveal a hint of the luxuriant garden that unfolds beyond. Behind the dark green foliage of *Salix hastata* 'Wehrhahnii' the delicate flowers of *Rosa* 'Nozomi', *Erinus alpinus* 'Dr Hähnle', *Hebe pimeleoides* 'Quicksilver', *Geranium cinereum* 'Ballerina' and other treasures await discovery below the graceful branches of *Prunus salicifolia* 'Pendula'.

Thirty years ago it was all very different. When my husband and I first saw the pair of cowman's cottages, they were ugly and derelict – we learned after we had bought them that the whole street was condemned and due to be demolished. The local council gave us and the other cottages on the hill a reprieve when convinced that we were going to make something of them, but the building society was less lenient and would not give us a loan; they looked upon us as two unusual and artistic people who would never finish what we had started. So we had to pay for the rebuilding of the cottages as we went along – it took us five years, evenings and weekends, and we did almost all of the work ourselves.

The garden then was just the area fronting the street. I laid the terrace and Alan built the staircase leading up into the two-acre field behind. There was nothing there but a couple of old apple trees, and for a peppercorn sum we were able to rent it from the farmer, for access only and for the boys to play in.

Thirteen years passed. Then Alan persuaded the local council to repair the old mill at the top of the field and to make under it a shelter for old people. The land was compulsorily purchased by the council and I was able to buy a fifth of an acre to make a garden.

At last I was to have my secret garden. But my husband and I separated and his health, never good, deteriorated, so I was the sole breadwinner

and bringer-up of children. I knew very little about plants when I started, and could only cope with a simple composition of shrubs and lawns.

Secluded the garden has always been, but it only started to become a real secret garden six years ago, when I retired from work and was able to devote my entire life to making the whole place more beautiful.

I knew then what I wanted. Increasingly I loved rare plants, not because they are rare, but because I find them much more beautiful. These were the plants I wanted to grow, and grey-leaved plants, and those with pale, delicate flowers and soft, flowing forms.

I knew too that I wanted a small pool, for the tranquil sound of trickling water. So with the help of a local designer lady I sketched out a place for it on a small terrace, the only level piece of ground in the whole of the secret garden, backed by a circular wall which Alan and I had built ourselves of old Suffolk bricks. Notcutts made the pool, and my designer friend helped me to find the right proportion of beds to lawns: in such a small space every foot is important.

Right at the beginning, the farmer had allowed us to dig out a channel round the back of the cottage to make it free-standing against the damp. I decided to break a door through the spare bedroom and build a bridge to span the gap – a sort

An intimate corner created in the shape once filled by an old apple tree, the curving, rope-like trunk of which is now the only reminder. Two attendant nymphs dream in the grotto's dappled shade, surrounded by *Cistus* 'Peggy Sammons', *Adiantum pedatum, Polystichum setiferum* and *Agapanthus praecox orientalis*, with hostas, epimedium, ivy and *Acer palmatum atropurpureum* in the background.

of Japanese-style Bridge of Sighs. It was a lovely, romantic feature, and I encouraged the wisteria to cascade towards it. Now the bridge has gone and a little white greenhouse has a taken its place; although it has brought the garden into the house and given me a welcome extra room, sometimes on summer evenings I remember with regret my rustic bridge and the shadows it cast on the lawn.

One of the appeals of the garden is that it is so high above the town. At the lowest level, a surprise awaits you, for as you inch your way round the branches of the old greengage tree (covered now with different clematis to disguise the amputation of some of its limbs), you find yourself on a narrow path overlooking my neighbours' gardens – you feel as if you were in a box at the theatre. On you go, past a bank full of alpines, up some steps, through an arch covered with *Clematis cirrhosa* and *Rosa* 'Kathleen Harrop', around the decorative old shed and back into the main garden again.

Behind the alpine bank, as an essential shelter against the gales that whistle down the valley, I have planted a *leylandii* hedge, which I keep slim and shapely to give the most room to my shade border – almost the only one in the garden. Here there are mainly grey-leaved plants and pale flowers: a weeping pear, a delicate white-flowered fuchsia, lysimachia, a convolvulus with white flowers and *Aconitum hemsleyanum*.

The other shade bed, further up the slope, has the feeling of a grotto, with the one surviving apple tree smothered in *Clematis montana*, and an *Acer grosseri* var. *hersii* as a new companion to replace the other apple, which fell down in a great storm. You must peer underneath to find the statue, the hostas and ferns, the trilliums, epimediums, *Uvularia grandiflora* and little hardy orchids.

In spring, this bed and the others will have bulbs – snowdrops, aconites, narcissi and species tulips. I don't like anything that is too big, or makes too much of a statement, like large-flowered clematis, the sharp leaves of iris, prickly berberis or the harsh foliage of potentilla. Everything must be flowing, softened by climbers or low-growing mounds and ribbons of foliage. At the top of the garden, before you go into the greenhouse and propagating area (hidden by a yew hedge), an archway is covered with two of the small-flowered clematis – creamy *C. rehderiana* and yellow, thick-petalled *C. tangutica*.

When it is in full beauty, I am most pleased with the bed here at the top of the garden: somehow the combination of daphnes,

The secret garden slopes down behind the house, towards neighbouring roofs and the river winding far below. In July this upper bed is painted in delicate, luminous shades of grey, pink and purple. *Rehmannia elata* and *Artemisia* 'Powis Castle' reach up between *Aster x frikartii* 'Mönch' and *Lavatera* 'Barnsley'; *Rosa* 'Aimée Vibert' and *R.* 'Penelope' add their scented flowers. The greenhouse lies behind, higher still.

ceanothus, ceratostigma, *Lilium regale, Solanum jasminoides* 'Album', felicias, *Zigadenus elegans* seems just right to my eye. But next year I will probably make some changes. It was a liberating moment to me when I visited the plantsman's garden a few miles away and he told me that to him every year was so important that he took things out and got rid of them. So now I do take things out – but I give them away, so I know they continue to thrive elsewhere.

I spend a lot of time in the greenhouse, and propagating. It's like looking after a nursery full of babies: they are always too hot, or too dry, or too damp. I love weeding, on my knees so that I'm within a few inches of the plants and can see their great beauty. Occasionally I sit under the old apple tree and think about the whole design, especially in the evenings when the light is changing and the plants take on different hues. In my life I have known much ill-health and some unhappiness; I am a solitary person by nature, and my great love affair has always been with my garden. I'm in love with my garden – it sounds rather strange, but it's true.

XI

INSTANT IMPRESSIONS

The raised level of the pond keeps it private from the street.

I N THE LATE WINTER of 1977 the garden at the Frick Collection in New York City, part of the newly constructed addition to the museum, existed only in the mind of Russell Page, who had been selected to design it. I was very young when I was interviewed by him for the job as gardener. He was so frightening and overwhelming I thought it best to agree with everything he said – when I had the chance to say anything at all. It was the right decision, and I got the job.

In the following weeks, as spring thawed the soil, the garden rapidly took shape. Working only from approximate drawings and memory, Russell laid out paths, lawns and beds. Truckloads of broad-leaved evergreens arrived – mountain laurel, white and pink azaleas, rhododendrons – making a bank of loose green and color against the dark north wall, beneath an elevated planter supported by hidden steel girders and filled with twelve tall Bradford pears fronted by Russian olive. Over a hundred 'Iceberg' roses arrived which were placed along the east wall beneath green trellises to be covered with pyracantha, *Clematis henryi, Clematis montana* var. *rubens* and *Akebia scandens*. These loose and informal plantings were accented by a disciplined structure at every level composed of sharply trimmed columnar yew, perfectly rounded mounds of Korean box-wood, and English box outlining the shape of every flowerbed and path.

The private world created by Russell Page is in direct contrast with the busy and eclectic collection of treasures inside the museum. His formal green space is not to be walked in but only viewed, like an Impressionist painting. The reticent planting, the clipped box edging and the rectangular pool perfectly complement the grand French style of the architecture, with its tall round-headed arches.

All the while the garden was taking shape, Russell, chain-smoking, waving his arms, drawing lines on notepaper, would expound his theories: don't be a snob about a particular flower or plant; use anything if it accomplishes the desired effect. Don't be afraid of formal elements: they give a garden structure, especially in the winter when this is most needed. Don't imagine a garden in two dimensions, plotted on grid paper as many landscape architects do. Consider carefully a garden's height and depth. Know the angles from which it will be viewed: the greatest designers were masters of perspective.

For me it was truly the education of a gardener. Russell's garden at the Frick was almost instantaneous, constructed in three short weeks. There were no opening ceremonies, no black-tie parties, no press releases. One day not there, it was suddenly present.

From the outset Russell made it clear that the garden he designed was not to be strolled through, nor visited by school groups or garden clubs, nor scampered over by would-be nature lovers with bare feet. The Frick garden would contrast, not compete, with what he termed the 'stunted travesty of an English eighteenth-century park' – namely Central Park, only half a block away. He was adamant that it should be devoid of human visitors – with the exception of a single gardener. To ensure this feeling of quiet and peace, he employed a crushed pebble path so 'if ladies with heels try to walk on it they will fall and break their necks'.

Trained as a painter, Russell wanted the Frick garden to be viewed, in his own words, 'like an Impressionist painting'. The French formal structure – learned from his years of association with Geoffrey Jellicoe and his post-war assignment restoring many of France's large formal parks – was to be slightly overgrown by shrubs, dappled by light, varied by swathes of soft color and animated by water covered with tropical lilies and lotus. Thick vines were trained along the limestone walls so they would support panicles of wisteria blossoms in spring and cool the walls during summer months. No one plant or feature should dominate. There is a niche, still unfilled, for a sculpture. He requested a Rodin.

If any one feature does dominate, it is the rectangular pool in the center of the lawn. Viewed from the middle window of the reception room, also part of the 1977 addition, the pool is the focus of attention. But from the street, through the wrought-iron gates, it is hardly visible; only a hint of water and some lily flowers show above the green lawn. This effect, accomplished by raising the garden three feet above the level of the street, was Russell's cleverest design trick. Using these two different points of view and manipulating the perspective, he essentially created two gardens.

The view from the interior through the three tall, arched doors is grand, formal and deliberately French. The addition itself was modelled on Le Grand Trianon at the Palace of Versailles. Russell selected the original color of the room, a strong hue that came to be called tomato-soup red, to contrast boldly with the green of the garden when viewed through the panes of glass. From this perspective one looks down upon the garden, and has the impression of man dominating nature. The pool is not natural; it is faced with 12-inch limestone, impeccably cut. The garden appears divided by a central axis which, if one turns around 180 degrees, is maintained by the central hall of the house. Clipped yews, the two mounds of Korean box, even the trees look strategically placed. The Frenchman's fear of nature, of a garden that has grown out of control, is thus assuaged. The perspective is that of an aristocrat – one feels admitted to an historical elite.

By contrast, the view from the street is populist. One looks into rather than down upon. This is Russell's secret garden, to be discovered by everyday passers-by. He planted climbing 'New Dawn' roses along the black iron fence to create an air of mystery'. At the back is a tall narrow green door that leads nowhere. Roses were to be allowed to run rampant, almost obscuring the garden, to cause one to stop and peep. There were to be no signs or indications of ownership, no botanical name-tags or plaques of donors, no dedications. It was a garden to stop by for one moment, in a busy city.

Through the years Russell's design has been altered remarkably little. The first thing to go was the tomato-soup red of the entrance hall, changed to a more conservative green. The climbing roses are gone because the swarthy ironworker who constructed the fence saw them one day as he passed in his truck, stopped and cut them down with his pocket knife. 'Roses are no good for the iron fence.' Metallurgists have pronounced his opinion correct. Plantings have altered, mainly due to the shade from the spreading trees, and there is a severity in New York's weather that Russell Page did not predict, The original scheme, the ideas of the designer, are all intact. But Russell as a plantsman has required some adaptation to achieve his intended effect. The tuberous begonias he imported withered in weeks under New York's summer heat. The trees soon shaded the 'Iceberg' roses, which were replaced by pink and white astilbes, and keeping an edge to clipped yews in a garden that gets four hours of sun at most and directional light at best, has been impossible. Presently, trimmed holly is being attempted as a replacement, but the jury is still out.

However, when the Sargeant's flowering cherry succumbed to disease, it was replaced by a crab apple of identical shape. If anything, the design of the garden, and Russell's reputation, have been canonized since his death. It is ironic, as this is an attitude with which he had no patience. He was a great advocate of change and growth. He believed that if a garden's structure was sound it would stand the test of time. When the life's work of many gardeners has been reduced to drawings and memories, Russell's Frick garden will survive in its beauty.

GALEN LEE, THE FRICK COLLECTION, NEW YORK CITY

XII

LEGACY OF A LEGENDARY GARDENER

Crinum moorei, one of the many reminders of the garden's creator.

IN FEBRUARY 1986, I was seeking not a garden but a home, something smaller, in town, convenient to my business. The modest gray-shingled Cape Cod house, on a small lot in Charlotte, North Carolina, had belonged to Elizabeth Lawrence, the renowned garden writer, plant collector and landscape designer who was perhaps the first person to write about gardening in the south-eastern United States.

I was told that, due to age and neglect, there were not many treasures left in the garden, and indeed on first sight it seemed a bleak, chaotic mass of overgrown and ordinary vines and weeds. Workmen and their debris took up residence, and the ravaged garden and the turmoil of drastic renovations to the house created a grim picture. Friends who visited my new home in those early months questioned my judgement.

A twisted wild cherry tree sprawled across the front face of the house; once a lovely pink rose had roamed through the canopy of the old tree, but now all that remained was one listless cane. A ragged *Camellia sasanqua* hedge, devastated by a brutal cold snap, ran along the front walk. It looked like jagged teeth. The main garden path lay undefined and overrun, ending under a clump of towering pines; periwinkle and ivy concealed the design and harmony of the native stone walls and paths and the empty brick-edged pond. Barely visible on the back wall was a bas-relief plaque of the Madonna and Child. Her pale, luminescent face promised me that there were surprises hidden there.

Miss Lawrence's niece wrote that the garden was her aunt's laboratory – for me it was to become a classroom. My previous gardening experience had been on a large, sunny piece of property where I could till and dig the borders with great abandon. This new garden would bring a world of other gardeners to me, drawn by the unique and cherished plants gathered by Miss Lawrence through friends, both nearby and from around the world. My life was to become, not simpler, but certainly enriched.

The secret of this garden was to be the many rare blooms that, with love and care, waited to reawaken in each season. Throughout that first winter, when venturing out amongst the mysterious winter foliage, I found a bounty of delicate flowers. My first prize was the astonishing *Adonis amurensis*, with its chrome-yellow blooms and feathery green foliage, thriving in the cold shadow of the pines. Then I saw the white, pink and plum *Helleborus orientalis* and the buttercup-like *Ranunculus ficaria* with its bright, rounded green leaves. There were fragrant daphnes with pink and white flowers, and sweet box (*Sarcococca humilis*) was already opening.

Friends asked if I had read Miss Lawrence's books. These became, and continue to be, my constant companions in my search for knowledge of further unfolding miracles.

As spring passed to summer, I was determined not to lose any of the plants that remained. Continuously, in the midst of an extended drought and soaring temperatures, I watered every square inch. More sun was brought into the garden by hard but careful pruning of the trees, shrubs and vines, and

very gently I began to cultivate the garden, hoping not to disturb any plants and bulbs that might still be hiding beneath the soil's surface.

Thus began my extraordinary experience of tending a garden that had outlived its maker. As I saw Miss Lawrence's plans for her garden unfolding throughout the seasons, her spirit seemed to linger. Once the antique 'Cemetary' rose matured to blossom, I was delighted to discover her intention that its flowers should match that of a rose climbing above it in a neighboring flowering quince.

Now, as I write in late winter, *Osmanthus* x *burkwoodii* brings in its fragrance, not long after the passing of the Algerian iris, one of Miss Lawrence's favorites which I have restored to the garden. A collection of magnolia will soon fill the sky with scent and color – white, pink, and deep rose – complemented by the 'Moerloosei' quince in white, brushed with pink.

In summer it is gratifying that the crinums have begun to bloom again, adding not only color but also fragrance and handsome foliage. Throughout this season, the Confederate

ABOVE: Spring blooms line the main path, opening out to a shaded glade with a raised pond, home to iris, water plants and koi. The beautiful *Aesculus parviflora* flowering in the background was planted by Elizabeth Lawrence. RIGHT: A mystery rose clambers up a flowering quince above the mixed border of *Gladiolus byzantinus*, yellow geum, *Iris sibirica* 'Caesar's Brother' and shasta daisies.

jasmine, which climbs forty or more feet in a pine, fills the garden with its sweet scent, delighting visitors and neighbors. In late summer two favorite highlights have come back to this secret garden – the mauve *Scilla scilloides* and the oxblood lily, *Hippeastrum advenum*, with its rich, deep red, miniature amaryllis-type blooms.

The garden continues to bring forth its hidden treasures. This year it was *Lycoris albiflora* in beautiful cream and coral shades, blooming in great profusion. The 'Old Blush' rose in the wild cherry tree (*Prunus serotina*) has now grown twenty feet or more at my front door; it is no longer just a memory. As I write, a new clump of mysterious bulbs has appeared at the base of the pine tree outside my window. Pearly buds wait to reveal themselves to me for the first time.

It seems I have neither a smaller home nor a simpler lifestyle. I have rooms, not only in my house but in my garden as well. Garden chores and responsibilities continue endlessly throughout the seasons, but then each year continues to bring forth delightful treasures and surprises.

LINDIE WILSON, CHARLOTTE, NORTH CAROLINA

GARDENS WITHIN GARDENS

A garden inclosed is my sister, my spouse; a spring
shut up, a fountain sealed.

From *The Song of Solomon*

XIII

BURIED IN A BROAD HILLSIDE

> *'Literally buried within the heart of
> this broad hillside is the secret garden, a
> small, snug area dug out of the slope
> and bounded on the upper side by a
> semi-circular stone wall.'*

SET IN THE gently rolling hills of south central Pennsylvania is a fifty-acre estate with gardens and ponds, farming, pasture- and woodlands, rural in atmosphere yet close to a thriving urban center. The house is early twentieth century, solidly built of the regional stone which sets the tone for the landscaped areas surrounding it. On the south-east side, an expansive lawn is terminated by a swimming pool, its surface mirroring a conservatory which in the summer is a changing and entertaining center and in the winter a cool greenhouse.

Opposite, a gentle hill rises to the north-west, and here a garden has recently been designed by the Delaware landscape architect William H. Frederick Jr. It is an area of softly curving grass paths and stone steps with a wide variety of trees, flowering shrubs, bulbs and perennials, where a dramatic display of color is apparent each month of the year.

Literally buried within the heart of this broad hillside is the secret garden, a small, snug area dug out of the slope and bounded on the upper side by a semi-circular stone wall. Entering the hillside garden and starting to climb, you approach the arch of a massive stone bridge, built to span a former natural dry gully, along a grass path of lush greenness bordered by red-stemmed dogwood and *Sedum sarmentosum*. As you reach the bridge and pass under its arch, a handsomely carved, gently splashing fountain appears, the focal

point of this garden. A brick path circles the fountain on all sides and then leads to large granite steps which curve along the wall before passing out of the secret garden and to the hillside once again. Along the steps a wooden bench has been designed to fit tightly against the arc of the wall.

As is the hillside itself, the secret garden is a twelve-month delight. When the calendar year begins and the days are short and cold, this sheltered spot catches the sun low in the sky, and the bench becomes a place to enjoy whatever warmth it may produce. The green branches of *Jasminum nudiflorum* cascade over the wall, and the eye focuses on the bark of a *Prunus* x *yedoensis* and the interesting shape of a weeping hemlock. Opposite the bench, the bridge itself commands absolute attention for the sweep of its curves, the color and pattern of the stone and its sheer massiveness. As you climb the curving steps to leave the garden, the bright red berries of *Ilex verticillata* 'Winter Red' stand out dramatically.

When the days turn warmer and spring is in the air, the wall is blanketed by yellow-flowering jasmine and miniature daffodils appear. May and June, of course, bring a profusion of color. Three *Daphne caucasica* lead the parade, followed by the fragrant *Rosa* 'Charles de Mills', a *Buddleja alternifolia* and numerous *Salvia* x *sylvestris* 'Indigo'. The walls of the bridge are bedecked on one side with

Along a velvet-carpeted lane lined with *Alchemilla mollis* the way ahead is clear – over the bridge towards a screen of hawthorn, prunus, sycamore, stewartia. The majestic stone bridge itself, modelled on one at Waterperry Gardens in Oxfordshire, England, was built by a local craftsman. No hint of what lies below, but beneath the low stone parapet a secret garden is concealed, carved out of the hillside.

a *Bignonia capreolata* and *Rosa* 'New Dawn', and on the other with a clematis and *R.* 'Graham Thomas'.

The heat of the summer is relieved by the shade of the over-arching cherry and a weeping beech looming behind the stone wall. The daphnes continue to put on a show and are joined by a ground cover of *Sedum* 'Vera Jameson'. Three tall hemerocallis provide almost constant color from July to October, while a bright blue clematis twines vigorously among the jasmine. It is this time of year when the fountain plays its role to the fullest, providing a soft sound for the ear, a sparkling treat for the eye, and an element of welcome coolness during the heat of the day.

The blooming of a border of *Aster* x *frikartii* 'Mönch' is a signal that the summer parade will shortly be over. While the hybrid roses continue to provide color, even their blooming has begun to wane, and it is apparent that the annual cycle of color will soon be at an end.

A casual observer of this secret garden might notice a certain English feeling to it. While this was not a motivating

The semi-circular garden opens out under the massive arch of the bridge. There are plants for every season: in winter when *Jasminum nudiflorum* opens its welcome flowers, through summer with *Rosa gallica* and *Daphne caucasica*, to the mellowing days of hemerocallis and *Sedum* 'Vera Jameson'. A bench is underplanted with vinca; above a fountain, box, saponaria and red switch-grass provide evergreen interest.

idea, the fact that two of the garden's most important elements have their origin in that country may contribute to the Anglican impression. The most significant structure here is the stone bridge, which was inspired by one in Waterperry Gardens in Oxfordshire – it was built by the ingenious landscape contractor who has done other work on the property but who has never before been asked to tackle the construction of such a bridge.

The fountain is a copy of one seen in a London garden center. When attempts to purchase the original proved fruitless, pictures and measurements were taken. We tried to have it carved in this country, but cost estimates were prohibitive, so we found a sculptor from the Bath region of England who carved the fountain from Portland stone both expeditiously and at an affordable price.

Although we did not intentionally attempt to create a replica of a typical English garden, the fact that it has so turned out makes it not only a source of peace and repose but also a living memory of our happy visits to that country.

LOUIS J. APPELL JR, YORK, PENNSYLVANIA

XIV

JARDIN DE FANTAISIE

The summer garden – a riot of colour in a woodland setting.

T HE FIGHTING in the last war left a trail of destruction throughout Normandy. On 12 August 1944, as the defeated army retreated, they set fire to the Château d'Harcourt. Its park had already suffered grievously as a battlefield – most of the trees had been mutilated or destroyed by shells and machine-gun fire, the glasshouses shattered and the parterres cratered by bombs.

Faced with such devastation, what was to be done? There was little choice. It was a case either of giving up all idea of re-surrecting a park which now had nothing to relate to but the burnt-out shell of its former château, or of facing up to disaster and setting out to endow the garden with a new and different splendour.

We took up the challenge. We planted trees, realigned avenues and re-adjusted the lie of the land. Then, with the utmost care, we chose a site for a new summer garden, con-cealed and enclosed by flowering shrubs and a hedge of Japanese quince. In its design we kept to a unit of measure which has been scrupulously observed in the relationship between the width of the *allées*, the diameter of the central roundel, and the width of the four rectangles. The great classical architects of the past have always respected such ground-rules, because they are based on human proportions, whereby the thickness of the wrist is half that of the neck and this in turn, is half that of the waist.

Such rules can never be absolutes when it comes to land-scape. They must be subject to nature and consult the *genius loci* – the slopes and the character of the terrain, the surround-ings, the orientation, the sight-lines, the prevailing winds, etc. It was La Fontaine who remarked of Le Nôtre that 'he had the ability to order nature; and nature obeyed him because he asked of it only what it was capable of giving'. So when it comes to landscape design, our personal preferences must bow to the will of nature. In the summer garden we created here, for instance, normally I would have laid it all out on one level. For the sake of convenience I respected the existing slopes, and to my surprise I found this produced an entirely happy effect. The first sight of this garden comes as an arrest-ing surprise, for you enter the garden along a path at the highest level. As you look down on the grass sward with its ribbons of flowers, the slope of the ground is entirely unexpected and, once in the garden, enables you to enjoy more easily the flowers on the lower levels.

A garden, like any other work of art, cannot ever spring from a purely cerebral conception or some magic formula. As Paul Valéry rightly judged, in creation a proper balance must be struck 'between knowledge, feeling and power'. And so too, in design, must a rhythm be established in its colours and its massing. So along the length of our borders a blue tint occurs at regular intervals, by the simple device of planting delphiniums and the later-flowering asters; likewise, the corners of the borders and the perimeter of the roundel are marked by pink impatiens. Binding the whole composition to-gether, blocks of similar colour are repeated on different

levels to provide links between the spring and summer gardens and the banks, and to give unity.

Perhaps the single most important element in gardens and parks is space. It is an expression of the invisible. The space at the heart of the summer garden plays a vital role, and the pink impatiens with which it is fringed is its diadem.

All the world's fine gardens are noted for the unity of their composition, invariably underpinned by one or more axes – those invisible lines on which everything else hangs. Here the four outer borders are laid along two axes, the termination of which is marked by stone benches formed from treads rescued from the château's destroyed grand staircase.

The architecture of a garden exists to provide a harmonious and living framework for the plants it harbours. The life of a garden depends on movement and change, the interplay of trees and shrubs and flowers, the thrust of growth to reach the light or to annexe space, an inexorable struggle in which only the fittest survive. In our summer garden, we respect the

Set apart from the ruins of a château, a garden rose from the ashes of the Normandy battlefield. Enclosed by trees and flowering shrubs, garlands of annual and perennial flowers lie scattered on the sloping ground – a careless rapture of planting subtly ordered by the rhythm of its colour and massing and carefully contained within a skilfully planned formal framework. It represents the triumph of hope.

whims of plants, never holding back the red malope or the pink cosmos that droop under their own weight onto the blue *Salvia farinacea*.

So often beauty in a garden comes not so much from something wholly exceptional as from the harmony we manage to compose from the unexceptional. Bedding plants can be too bland or vulgar, beautiful flowers too grand or vigorous. In our summer garden, the severity of the framework is always tempered by a seeming disorder in the planting. It is this contrapuntal rhythm which produces equilibrium.

The park and garden we chose to create in the aftermath of the Normandy campaign was part traditional, part new. The tradition we espoused was the refusal to be overcome by events, however terrible they had been. After all, a beautiful garden should be reward enough. We kept in our minds the words of Simone Weil, who died during the last war: 'The evil that is everywhere can only be diminished by focusing on the perfection of something in itself beautiful.'

Duc d'Harcourt, Pavillon de Fantaisie, France

XV

THE RECTOR'S SECRET

Architectural *Fatsia japonica* add drama to the keyhole entrance.

At STANCOMBE the house stands high, looking southwards over undulating countryside; to the north, the higher edge of the Cotswolds provides shelter from icy winds. Cows and their calves graze just outside the house, below a Regency fence. There, the ground slopes down into a deep valley which folds round a nearby spur and disappears. On top of the spur, surrounded on three sides by sweet chestnuts and cedars, a terraced garden faces the house. The planting here is formal, restrained in colour to blend into the surrounding countryside; even in winter there are subtle shades of pink, blue and deep red in the newly planted pattern-borders. At the head of the garden, a pavement of pale grey and rose-pink bricks imitates the design of the Roman mosaic I dug up some years ago.

A deer fence descends from the east side of the formal garden into the wooded valley below. If you have not been here, you are sure to be drawn to take this route. You will come on a narrow flagstone path winding down, past trees entwined with rambler roses, until the entrance to the grottoes suddenly appears. A large stone dog – Cerberus, guardian of the Underworld – watches as you pass by. Venturing through the series of tunnels, you find yourself in another world. This is Stancombe's secret garden.

Its centrepiece is a lake surrounded by shrubs, rushes, ferns, gunnera and hedges of box and yew; to the south stands a neo-classical Greek temple. This garden, with its follies, reminds you of Egypt, China and Greece – it was in fact the creation of the Reverend Purnell-Edwards, who owned Stancombe in the early nineteenth century. A keen gardener and traveller who found inspiration in faraway places, he built grottoes and tunnels with doors that could be kept locked, and placed there strange objects (whales' vertebrae) with the help of soldiers recently demobbed from the Napoleonic Wars. His wife was stout, and therefore unable to manage the steep path down to the lake, let alone squeeze through the narrow grotto entrance. The story goes that the Reverend was carrying on an illicit love-affair with a local gypsy girl and planned his secret garden as a safe trysting-place. Was the Greek temple his folly of follies?

I love this place, with its romantic atmosphere and its ever-changing moods that vary with the season and the time of day. Light plays a fascinating role here and can produce magical effects. Two Roman villas lie hidden underground; there are no plans to excavate them, so their relics remain undisturbed, and contribute to the feeling of mystery. Over the years, my late husband Basil and I added to the follies. A large stone wild boar, whom we call Cornelius, taken from a cast at the Uffizi in Florence, now reclines at the end of a small peninsula on the lake. He gives the impression of relaxed supremacy, as if this has always been his domain.

Spring, with so much promise in the air, is my favourite time here. It is a thrill to see, as early as January, the first snowdrops, followed by sheets of primroses and bluebells in the adjoining woods: life itself beginning anew. The birds

seem particularly happy and noisy with their lovely songs. Later in May I hope for the glimpse of a fox or even a family of them. Rabbits and squirrels abound (should one love or hate them? They are so pretty, yet so destructive). This is the time when wildfowl fly in, looking for nesting sites, and pairs of pochards, pintails and mandarin ducks come to visit from the Slimbridge Wildlife Reserve nearby. Except for the mallards, they never stay, and I suspect the aggressive coots to be the culprits – they regard the lake as their territory. By now the large clumps of *Gunnera manicata* are unfurling their huge leaves by the water's edge.

Summer comes and passes pleasantly with all the lushness it can muster. The ferns are at their best and the Wichuraiana and other rambler roses are in flower high in the trees, the air heavy with their scent. In the lake the herons are busy fishing for the plentiful golden orfe; they wait with endless patience for their catch, but what a sight to behold when they open their great wings and slowly lift off into the air.

August is the month I like least: flies descend on man and beast and spoil all outdoor activities. The roses have long finished blooming and the foxgloves, such a feature earlier on, sway sadly with only a few blooms left high on their stems.

Hoar frost invests the secret garden with the staccato brilliance of Vivaldi's 'Winter'. ABOVE: The elegant neo-classical temple, built as a love nest in the early nineteenth century, commands the tree-fringed lake. In the foreground a newly planted trachycarpus will replace the older specimen. RIGHT: The boar, named Cornelius, stands guard on his peninsula behind a rampart of clipped yew.

On hot days you can still plunge into the water for a refreshing swim, but as the days grow shorter, there is a certain nip in the air and another treat in store: the lovely autumn has arrived. Soon the leaves begin to change colour to display the most glorious hues. Acers, beeches and liquidambar are particularly brilliant – I cannot help feeling sorry to see the autumn gales destroy this spectacle, ripping the leaves from their branches and hurling them into the air, before coming to rest on the ground or on the lake where, for a while, they spoil the reflected image of the beauty above. There is a special satisfaction in walking, ankle-deep, through rustling leaves giving off their unmistakable smell.

Whether working or wandering in the garden, I often think of those master musicians of the eighteenth century – Haydn and Vivaldi – and their interpretations of the seasons. With the coming of winter, I naturally think of Vivaldi. His staccato 'Winter' conjures up all sorts of images of ice and snow and icicles, giving us the dramatic sight of a landscape transformed by hoar frost into a fairyland.

Folly or no, we cannot but feel grateful to the Reverend for planning this secret garden. A place of enduring charm, it contains more secrets than he could have realized.

GERDA BARLOW, STANCOMBE PARK, GLOUCESTERSHIRE

XVI

SYLVIA'S GARDEN

Sylvia Compton's secret wrought in the gates to her garden.

'Who is Silvia? what is she
That all our swains commend her?'

I WAS TOO YOUNG to know if Shakespeare's immortal words encouraged my father to design a secret garden for my mother in 1930, but they make a fitting introduction to my piece.

A secret garden implies that you do not know what you are going to find – an enclosure hidden from view until the last moment. Open the gate and suddenly all is revealed. Perhaps subconsciously, the quiet and peaceful enclosure of Sylvia's Garden, carefully screened from the rest of the gardens at Newby, inspired my wife to introduce the charming iron gates, carved with my mother's initials, SC, into the three entrances. With well over 110,000 visitors coming to Newby each year, the gates now also carry a message which reads: 'At the request of our visitors, this memorial garden is a place to be enjoyed in peace and quiet. No children or prams please.'

In 1930, of course, there were no such problems, and luckily for my father no shortage of labour or money. Much has been written elsewhere about his grand design for Newby; he was certainly influenced by Hidcote in the concept of a central axis, a corridor with garden rooms off it. Sylvia's Garden was the first of these. The design was for a sunken garden in a square enclosure surrounded by well-clipped hedges of yew; the rest of the garden was to be on three levels with a simple, classical pattern of beds, the paths paved with brick and stone, and a carved Byzantine stone grinder as the centre point. It has been said that the design echoes an Adam ceiling, and my father may indeed have been guided by the classical proportions he saw all around him in the house.

When he died, we decided to replant the whole of Sylvia's Garden, as most things were long past their best and the soil needed renewing. The original design had eight beds surrounding the stone grinder in the centre; my wife thought it would be more effective and less fussy to remove the diagonal paths which ran from the four corners, to give more space in just four beds. So it has proved, but we made one mistake. The centre of each bed was planted with *Rosa* 'Nozomi', top-worked to form standards, glorious umbrellas of pink standing over the misty mauve of *Calamintha nepeta*. Not so. 'Nozomi', in my opinion, hates being suspended in mid-air and will not respond to loving attention – so out with 'Nozomi' and in with that old favourite *R.* 'Ballerina' instead.

LEFT: Looking towards the steps which climb eastwards from the Byzantine corn grinder – surrounded by *Calamintha nepeta* – *Argyranthemum foeniculaceum, Potentilla fruticosa* 'Daydawn' and fine-foliaged grey and green plants spill over paving stones. OVERLEAF: An elegant pair of dogs guards the approach beyond the hydrangeas flanking the path. Two Arizona cypresses stand sentinel at the exit.

In autumn the sunken garden, enclosed by clipped
yew hedges, glows with mellow colour. A standard
rose 'Ballerina' is surrounded by pink argyranthemum, with pink monbrieta in the foreground. At all
times of the year, foliage plants with wide, subtle variations in colour and texture play a role as important as
that of the flowering plants.

The design of the garden is perfectly balanced and symmetrical, so the planting scheme within it had to conform. The patterns of colour complement each other in corresponding beds and on corresponding levels. The colour schemes throughout are soft and subtle, for the spirit of the garden is peaceful. Just a few stronger colours have been allowed to appear at the back of the garden against the dark background of yew – the *basso profundo* of the orchestra.

My wife has an unerring eye for colour and form, and I have studied plants all my life; this should make a happy and successful combination. Usually it does, but sometimes we disagree and then she always wins – rightly so, as it is her artistry that has produced such a beautiful picture.

The planting has been planned to provide colour and interest throughout the year; a far cry from my father's day. He chose plants that would be at their best for York Races in May, when his visitors came to admire them. Now Sylvia's Garden is full of charm and colour from April to October.

In early spring bulbs have their say, though the pheasants do their best to keep them silent. *Tulipa kaufmanniana* and its hybrids, also the lovely *T. clusiana* and the double early hybrid *T.* 'Peach Blossom' begin the floral display, followed by grape hyacinths – the pale blue *Muscari azureum* and the pretty but unkempt tassel hyacinth *M. comosum*. Iris and alliums are not far behind, notably *Allium aflatunense* with its star-shaped pink-purple flowers; nor must I forget the pasque flower, *Pulsatilla vulgaris*, with its blue-purple anemone flowers.

In early May a host of other plants burst into bloom to replace the fading bulbs: the cranesbills, *Geranium malviflorum*, *G. sanguineum*, and its natural variety from Lancashire, *G. sanguineum* var. *striatum*, *G. cinereum* and its beautiful cultivar 'Ballerina'. The creeping Jacob's ladder, *Polemonium reptans*, with mid-blue, saucer-shaped flowers in loose panicles, is nearby. Then there are those delightful members of the cress family, *Aethionema* 'Warley Ruber' (commemorating Ellen Willmott, who made the Rock Garden here), and alyssum in its pale yellow form follows on, now called *Aurinia saxatilis* var. *citrina*. A stronger yellow tone comes from the flowers of *Euryops acraeus*, softened by its silvery leaves. Sadly it is sometimes stolen, but we keep spares to replace it.

Other noteworthy rock plants for the edges of the beds are *Lithodora diffusa* 'Heavenly Blue' and its close lime-tolerant relative *Moltkia* x *intermedia*, *Dryas octopetala*, the pretty mountain avens indigenous to these islands, and *Anthemis punctata* subsp. *cupaniana*, an attractive relative of the chrysanthemum. A superb plant for breaking a straight line cascading over the walls is the unusual *Sphaeralcea munroana*, a globe mallow from North America with orange-pink petals and a deeper centre. Its laciniate leaves are attractive too.

For taller effects, my wife has made much skilful use of the chrysanthemum tribe. We take cuttings each year of the best of the 'Canary Island' cultivars – *Argyranthemum* 'Mary Wootton' is pale pink, 'Vancouver' deeper pink, 'Jamaica Primrose' pale yellow, and 'Snowflake' as white as it sounds. *A. foeniculaceum* and *A. maderense*, with blueish leaves and yellow flowers, also play a valuable part in the colour scheme; this excellent plant was reintroduced into cultivation by my son James. On the top level, the luscious hybrids of *Paeonia lactiflora* provide rich colour and scent at the height of summer: *P.* 'Bowl of Beauty', *P.* 'Sarah Bernhardt', *P.* 'Shirley Temple' and *P.* 'Duchesse de Nemours' are the best here.

I cannot leave the scene without describing a few of the best foliage plants, like the salvias, with their rich variations in colour. The common sage is such a useful plant in several forms, notably *Salvia officinalis* 'Icterina', with pale-green and yellow leaves, and *S. o.* 'Purpurascens', a good purple. Then the wormwoods provide excellent silver foliage – *Artemisia absinthium* 'Lambrook Silver' and *A. ludoviciana* 'Silver Queen'.

At the top level, marking the four corners, the variegated snowberry, *Symphoricarpos orbiculatus* 'Foliis Variegatis' gives light and strength against the dark yew. For infilling, a useful foliage shrub is *Hypericum* x *moserianum* 'Tricolor', its leaves edged with pink and yellow; another hypericum, *H. olympicum* f. *uniflorum* 'Citrinum', with pale lemon flowers and greyish leaves, complements the brick walls beneath the apricot flowers of *Potentilla fruticosa* 'Daydawn'.

I must stop before I give away all the garden's secrets. The birds are singing and the scent of the flowers invites you in. Just open Sylvia's gate and walk quietly to the seat at the back. The garden will tell you the rest.

ROBIN COMPTON, NEWBY HALL, NORTH YORKSHIRE

XVII

FOUNTAIN AND ROSES

A daring outburst of ice-blue iris among orange asclepias.

MY EARLIEST RECOLLECTION of a garden was my mother's in California. Our yard was small, with just enough room for an old apricot tree and the beautiful rich borders she had planted around it. At the time the apricot tree was the center of my brothers' and my life: we picnicked beneath its canopy, devoured its sweet fruit, climbed among its branches and dreamed of foreign lands. Mother's borders were made up of calla lilies, acanthus, iris, camellias and fuchsias; in the corner was a tall branched poinsettia. We ate artichokes and boysenberries she had grown, wonderful guavas and, of course, the apricots. We learned how to watch the ripening of the fruit to catch it at its most delectable moment, full of sweet nectar, the skin just blushing, highlighting its apricot flesh.

When I was thirteen, we moved. Mother's new garden was mainly lawn, edged with ajuga and ice plant for low maintenance and surrounded by a glorious array of fruit trees and a large golden acacia. I remember rising early and finding my mother deep in thought in her new garden. When I asked her to tell me what she was thinking about, she told me that smelling the early morning air, watching the birds at first light and seeing the sun catch the tops of the trees calmed her and filled her with the wonder of life. I have carried her words with me and think of them often.

When I married and moved to New York State, I was fortunate

The romance of the rose – fragrant flowers spill over the edges of a path meandering through the rose garden to the fountain garden beyond. White *R.* 'Madame Hardy', entwined with *Clematis* 'Etoile Violette', leads on to low-growing pink 'Jenny Duval', then, on the right, to 'Tricolore de Flandre' and the darker purple 'Tuscany' with *R.* 'Alba Semi-plena' and 'Maiden's Blush' in the background.

enough to have a country home where I could garden. Although I had studied botany in college, my gardening was experimental, stimulated by my love of flowers. In time, my husband and I visited England specifically to see the gardens there. We were impressed and inspired by the tradition of garden rooms at Hidcote and Sissinghurst. On our return I engaged Hitch Lyman and together we developed a series of gardens to fit the landscape of our present home.

We created two secluded areas, the fountain garden and a rose garden. One enters the fountain garden through a Canadian hemlock hedge twelve feet high. The Mediterranean feeling of this garden is suggested by the use of bright annuals, clematis, and small hardy plants displayed in Italian terracotta pots. The seeds from the flowers have fallen between the paving stones and reflower annually as a reminder of years past. In the early morning my children and I often breakfast at the small stone table near the fountain.

Each year the exotics in the pots vary – once *Gloriosa superba* (syn. *G. rothschildiana*) twisted through the hedge from its container, now there are moonflowers (*Calonyction aculeatum*), bougainvilleas, *Clematis florida* 'Sieboldii', lantana, tuberoses, scented geraniums and *Tibouchina urvilleana* (syn. *T. semidecandra*). My favorites are the poppies, Johnny jump-ups, *Dianthus deltoides* 'Albus' and *Myosotis alpestris*

which grow between the paving stones. There is something wonderfully calming about this circular space. Stepping onto the smooth cobblestones surrounded by the tall dark hedge of the roundel, the focus of one's thoughts becomes the soothing sound of the water.

The fountain garden leads into the sequestered rose garden. Through a narrow opening in the hemlock hedge a metal gate swings open to reveal a romantic fantasy of old garden roses. The heady fragrance of the Albas, Gallicas and Damasks delights the senses in June. *Dianthus deltoides* 'Albus', *Corydalis cheilanthifolia, Papaver rhoeas* 'Mother of Pearl', *P. dubium, P. ruprifragum* and *P. commutatum* sprout up between the stones under the pastel roses.

The main walkway is on an axis with the fountain but there are two side paths. As one meanders past the rose 'Maiden's Blush', a corner may be turned which has shielded *R.* 'Cardinal de Richelieu', a pale creamy-yellow variety of *Paeonia peregrina, Artemisia* 'Powis Castle' and *Nicotiana langsdorffii*. Here 'Félicité Parmentier', 'Aglaia' and 'Bobbie James' are worked into the surrounding tapestry willow hedge.

RIGHT: The fountain garden is entered through an arch in the stepped, clipped Canadian hemlock hedge. ABOVE: Cobbles and paving stones, laid in a circle, radiate from the fountain. The pots surrounding it and the perimeter are filled with seasonal plants. *Buddleja davidii*, attracts butterflies in the background, *Hydrangea macrophylla* and red cabbage provide purple accents and pelargoniums a splash of purest red.

Every few steps another secret unfolds, for this is a wild and unruly rose garden with scented geraniums, trautvetteria, *Geranium phaeum* 'Album' and *Nectaroscordum siculum* subsp. *bulgaricum*. *Rosa* 'Jeanne d'Arc' forms an arch over Rosa Mundi, which is tucked beneath a planting of 'Alba Semiplena' and 'Madame Legras de Saint Germain'. 'Belle Amour' is underplanted with pale pink pansies to match the color of its fallen petals.

The ramblers 'Gardenia', 'Rambling Rector' and 'The Garland' spread wilfully; most are not hardy in our area and are untied from the hedges and bedded down for winter with burlap protection. They look like serpents covered with snow, mysterious winter sculptures hidden beyond the hemlock and its secret gate. The hedge is a mixture of *Salix purpurea, S. alba* var. *sericea* (syn. *S.a.* f. *argentea)*, *S. elaeagnos, Hipphophaë rhamnoides* and *Buddleja alternifolia* 'Argentea'.

These are my secret gardens, romantic hideaways described in the fairytales I dreamed of as a child in my mother's apricot tree, the gardens which calm me and fill me with the wonder of life.

LAURA FISHER, KATONAH, NEW YORK STATE

XVIII

IN A COOL CLIMATE

Hot colours for an October wedding – dahlias, molucella, lilies.

I WAS A YOUNG BOY in New Zealand when our family moved to Napier, a prosperous east coast town that had been all but destroyed by a severe earthquake five years before. In the mid-1930s, this flower-filled town was being rebuilt in the current Art Deco style with a unique marine parade as its showpiece feature – a sort of small town antipodean *Promenade des Anglais*, with smooth lawns, shrub borders, band stand, pergola and fountain, bisected by paths and beds of vivid annuals and dominated by towering Norfolk pine.

A few blocks back from this focus of civic pride, among cleaned lots awaiting new buildings, stood the brick shell of the Presbyterian Church, our family church, unfinished but, because of the 'quake, condemned. While we attended services in a temporary wooden building, it was this Gothic ruin that fascinated me. Birds flew through the empty windows, while among the jumble of arches and columns smashed in the foundations grew a jungle of weeds. Seedling acacia reached for the sky amongst wild fennel, and smothering German ivy turned the trails into a green labyrinth. I am sure I followed the other boys through the broken door and down a pile of loose rubble into this spooky and forbidden playground. Even today I only have to catch the rank smell of crushed senecio or pungent fennel to remember that walled hideaway – my first secret garden.

Blooming for a summer party, the walk-in cooler is filled with a riotous assembly of yellows, pinks and purples – a fleeting reunion of local mixed roses, sunflowers from California, delphiniums, hybrid gerbera and gladioli from Holland, cymbidium orchids and leucospermum from New Zealand. Outside it may be scorching or snowing – in this garden room the temperature is a constant 45°F (7°C).

I have enjoyed the encounter many times in my life, in every country I have visited – the strange gate yielding to pressure, the lure of water splashing on stone, the overgrown disorder of what-used-to-be – evidence, if any were needed, that gardening man chooses to contain his Eden. A door I opened from within the great Cathedral of Assisi led into just such a measured space. Dark magnolia contained the sunny yard where a terracotta figure of St Francis above the fountain spread wide his arms to the white doves, and yes, of course, there was the fragrance of thyme and lavender, and bees buzzing. Italians have the confident style of long familiarity with garden rooms.

From the splash of water and color in the Alhambra, the Moorish influence travelled throughout the New World; from Mexico to Argentina one discovers private gardens where each hacienda encloses its fountain, trees and flowers in a personal sanctum. I have seen how the Japanese condense the essence of a garden with great serenity into any available place, using carefully selected plants and moss, rock and gravel. These have been important discoveries. Generations of English gardeners have absorbed and adapted the garden room in their own charming ways. Within mellow walls of brick, boxwood or clipped yew, still pools reflect arched doorway or topiary beast, and subtle

One of the most enjoyable features of the secret garden is its lay-out into rooms. Walking from the formal to the rose garden, you climb three steps past pink azaleas flanked by 'Mount Fuji' cherry trees. There are over 100 rose bushes in more than thirty varieties, primarily Hybrid Teas. The beds surrounding the Four Seasons statues on the perimeter of the rose garden are planted with Iceland poppies in wonderland pink shades, with an outer border of imperial blue pansies. The same holds true for the center bed with its globe-shaped sundial. The theme varies, year to year.

The perennial borders, set off from the rest of the secret garden by two long rows of American box some six feet high and three feet wide, are my favorites, bursting with color in an unstructured manner – more English than England. The narrow border together with our desire to have everything creates an unusual array of blooms, as the normally short flowers stretch upwards in search of light.

ABOVE: An English border in an American walled garden. Pacific hybrid delphiniums, foxgloves, lupins and double peonies – with flax, nigella and Iceland poppies for ephemeral beauty – display their summer wares before a hedge of American box with lilac above. RIGHT: A tunnel of American and English box, backed by pale pink flowering cherry trees, signals the entrance to the walled garden.

Beyond the perennial border, lilacs tower above the American box as if trying to get an aerial view. An *allée* of alternating red cedar and 'Kwanzan' cherries, bordered by now-tamed English box, leads to a wisteria-covered pergola, a wonderful place to hide and read. As you walk down the *allée*, your eye is drawn left and right across an expanse of grass to what we call the long borders, or shrub borders, edged with daffodils planted in 1925. I refer to the *allée* as our old-world walk, and it feels so good to be strolling along, hearing the wild turkeys gobbling in the distance. In the early morning the geese honk as they wing their way to the James River a short distance away, and the whiporwills are joined by many other birds to add to the symphony of music and color.

Last year during Garden Week in Virginia I heard more than one person exclaim: 'Why is this garden so hidden? Where is the main house? Let's keep it our secret.'

CHARLES L. REED JR, RICHMOND, VIRGINIA

FORMAL ENCLOSURES

Stretch out the lines of every avenue
With spreading trees in many stately rows;
Display the parterres and the shady walks,
The sloping greens, the ponds and water-works.

John Clerk of Penicuik (1676–1755): from *The Country Seat*

XX

ENCLOSED BUT NOT EXCLUSIVE

The heart of the garden – a rhythmical pattern of box and yew.

Our garden has grown slowly, layer by layer, over the past decade. Early on the idea came to me that it should be allowed to develop of its own accord, at its own pace.

I had decided to lay a path, which would also act as demarcation for the beds I planned, but when I discovered that a mass of old cobbles – now highly prized but disregarded then – were to be thrown out by local builders, the opportunity to use these throughout the garden was too good to miss. Each stone was carefully selected and worked into shape before taking its allotted place in the overall scheme.

I started the planning and planting of the garden on the side of the main elevation of the house. In the elliptical front bed, bordered with box, I planted 'The Fairy' roses. A cobbled path leads to the bridge which I designed and built in the romantic style. The bridge itself then needed a *raison d'être*, so we dug a moat. This was bounded on one side by an artificial mound planted with trees and rose hedges so as to combine shade and shelter with flowering splendour. Sandstone blocks from demolished farmhouses nearby formed a retaining wall around the hill. For the backdrop planting, which extends as far as the inner courtyard, I have chosen a number of rarities such as *Cornus kousa*, davidia, catalpa, gleditsia, *Robinia pseudoacacia*, liquidambar, *Quercus palustris, Fagus sylvatica* 'Pendula' and *Ulmus glabra* 'Wredei'.

A clipped parterre of box with a central tiered yew fountain has been trimmed into shape over twenty years. The intricate, geometric design has an almost Elizabethan simplicity emphasized by the infill of gravel and cobbles. Over the archway, Virginia creeper makes a green curtain flaming to scarlet in autumn. Cobblestones are laid in swirling patterns to articulate the pathways.

The bridge marks the entrance to the heart of the garden – the box parterre, encircled by cobbles, where the many clipped pyramids and balls create an evergreen pattern that is cool yet dramatic at all times of the year.

After circling the central box bed, the path straightens before passing under an archway hung with Virginia creeper into the courtyard garden, where in a raised bed hybrid azaleas and species of wild rhododendron – *R. impeditum* and *R. yakushimanum* – hold court in shades of lilac and rose. Around the pool are bulbs and summer- and autumn-flowering shrubs with fresh yellow, pink and purple flowers, and between these I have placed interesting stones. The pool itself, strewn with water-lilies, reflects the changing sky and the leisurely activity of the goldfish. Each year the two beds in front of the pool are planted anew with annual summer flowers.

Throughout the garden, flowers and shrubs have been introduced to refresh and loosen the formality and discipline imposed by the dominant box topiary and by the river of cobblestones that unites and unifies its different parts.

We are screened from our immediate neighbours but on one side can be overlooked from the footpath which skirts the property and on the other from open pastureland grazed in summer by cattle. So we have a feeling of enclosure but not of exclusion from the outside world.

In contrast to the box parterre, whose formal architectural shapes may be glimpsed in the background, the planting beside the bridge is romantic and colourful. A gleaming shoal of goldfish swims in the shadow of the low-arched bridge, among the mats of water-lilies, surrounded by stone-edged beds of marigold and larkspur, rudbeckia, delphiniums and the deep pink flowers of *Buddleja* 'Royal Red'.

Each season brings its own reward. In May we look forward to the flowering of the box, rhododendrons and azaleas, and in the succeeding months to the spectacle of the roses, herbaceous flowers and summer-blooming shrubs. In autumn the crowning moment is the sight of the Virginia creeper forming a triumphal arch to the courtyard. Passing under its flame-coloured leaves, you will notice a semicircular recess in the sandstone wall, edged with pointed-leaved ivy, into which we plan to place the impression of an old wayside shrine. As I sit here in the early evening after a perfect summer's day, this small enclosed space seems wrapped in a protective cloak of age and secrecy.

KARL ARTMEYER, HORSTEL RIESENBECK, GERMANY

XXI

ROOMS FOR IMPROVEMENT

'The area we planned to cultivate was about two acres, partly walled, and set in ten acres of pastureland. We spent the first months hacking our way through the undergrowth trying to find something worth keeping. Slowly the grim truth dawned – there was practically nothing to save . . .'

WE FOUND the house with the help of an Ordnance Survey map and a pair of binoculars, after a chance remark at a party had set us on the trail – the owners were thinking of emigrating. Six months later Rofford Manor was ours. Friends thought the move sheer folly, and even our children, who we had hoped were too young to notice, regarded their new surroundings with undisguised horror. The previous occupants claimed to have planted a conifer wherever they felt a draught, and after a quarter of a century this policy had proved most effective: the house was totally hidden from view, and the garden was certainly secret.

The area we planned to cultivate was about two acres, partly walled, and set in ten acres of pastureland. We spent the first months hacking our way through the undergrowth trying to find something worth keeping. Slowly the grim truth dawned – there was practically nothing to save, only a mature robinia, two laburnum trees, two viburnums, an ancient philadelphus and some rhubarb.

We gritted our teeth and sent for the chainsaws and the bulldozer – the house was suddenly filled with light. Then we weedkilled the forest floor, levelled the area, divided the garden into compartments – guided by the walls – and planted a quarter of a mile of yew hedging to complete the rooms. We seeded a lawn of football-pitch dimension and sat back to enjoy our newly created garden. The resulting *tabula rasa* was immensely disappointing, to say the least, closely resembling a windswept wasteland.

Help came in the form of Michael Balston via an article by Christopher Lloyd in *Country Life* describing a garden Michael had designed that was filled with the most exciting plants, shrubs and trees. This was exactly what our garden lacked, but it was six years before anything was finally planted. There was much to do first!

The large lawn was separated from the house by a narrow, sunless, north-facing terrace. This was extended by making a rose garden: eight beds filled with white roses, flowering shrubs and perennials set in a large area of stone paving. We now had somewhere sheltered and sunny to sit, reasonably close to the house. Then came an awkward area on the east side of the house below a herb garden we had planted with the help of Simon Hopkinson from Hollington Nurseries. We separated the two areas with box and used green and yellow plants, with blue provided by *Campanula poscharskyana* 'Stella', *Lavandula* 'Hidcote' and *Viola labradorica*. In the centre is a square of grass containing a knot of box filled with *Santolina neapolitana*.

The gravelled entrance courtyard was planned as a green room surrounded by pleached limes. The vegetable garden lies to the far side and a small garden leads off the yard on the west side of the house; this continues the green theme, with a raised pool surrounded by box, gravel paths and lots of pots.

The swimming pool is perhaps the most secret place here, effectively a garden within a garden and contributing an element of suprise. The atmosphere here is quite different from

the other areas. It is surrounded on two sides by high stone and brick walls built, according to an inscription, in 1742; the third side is enclosed by a pavilion constructed from the same materials, with a central arch leading to the rose garden. The room is completed by a yew hedge along the north side, with a path to the herb garden through what, given a few more growing years, will be a yew arch. Although the pool is barely thirty yards from the house, it is totally hidden by the yew.

We wanted the area to look as natural as possible so that it could be enjoyed throughout the year. The pool is lined with grey marble tiles which make the water a subtle shade of blue, and old York stone paving has been used up to the water's edge and as flooring for the pavilion. Four raised stone beds support the iron framework of pergolas along either side of the pool. The planting has a slightly exotic feel, with pink and purple flowers from spring until the first frosts. In the centre of each raised bed grows the purple-flowered *Hibiscus syriacus* 'Duc de Brabant', surrounded by pale pink hardy *Fuchsia* 'Susan Travis'. These beds were replanned last year in colours that mirrored the *Buddleja davidii* 'Royal Red' and *Crinum* × *powellii* planted at the west-facing end of the pool. We had to abandon the previous planting of *Romneya* × *hybrida* because every time a stem was knocked it turned bright yellow and

ABOVE: The enclosed swimming-pool garden is dominated by raised beds of *Romneya* x *hybrida* backed by *Vitis coignetiae* on pergolas. The arched entrance wall is lined with box pyramids and pillars of *Myrtus communis*. RIGHT: A green and yellow garden at the north-east corner. *Rosa gallica* brightens the foreground, *R.* 'The Garland' and 'Wedding Day' grow on arbours in the rose garden beyond.

died. It now looks much better in the rose garden, where it can flop as it pleases, completely undisturbed.

The pergolas, the same shape as the arch through the centre of the pavilion, are covered with *Vitis coignetiae*, creating wonderful tunnels of shade along either side of the pool. They need frequent clipping to keep their curved shape, but the effect is well worth the effort. A catalpa is centred on the pavilion at the far end of the pool, and enclosing each side of the seating area are *Crambe cordifolia* and *Clematis recta*. These two are supposed to produce their froth of white flowers simultaneously – some years it works, sometimes they miss each other.

The path through the yew is flanked by the lush foliage of *Acanthus mollis* and *Rheum palmatum* 'Atrosanguineum', and *Corylus maxima* 'Purpurea', *Cotinus coggygria* and *Acer palmatum* 'Atropurpureum' add splashes of purple. The acer barely tolerates our limy soil but fortunately is not required to fill a large space – although it looks well enough, it has hardly grown in five years.

The walls are covered with roses, pale pink 'François Juranville' and 'New Dawn' at each end, graduating to dark crimson 'Guinée' in the corner. In front of this stands a majestic clump of *Cortaderia selloana* 'Sunningdale Silver', which makes a wonderful focal point but has to be cut well

back away from the seat to spare unsuspecting guests the disfiguring red weals that appear on contact with its innocent-looking leaves.

The pergolas are populated with tiny wrens; they nest among the dense foliage of the vines, along with a pair of bunting whose plaintive song haunts the area all summer. Butterflies of every hue cover the buddleja and the sedum that grow at its feet. Hidden away from the world, there are times when the swimming pool garden feels almost Mediterranean. As it becomes increasingly sheltered and enclosed, the scent is held, particularly after the sun has heated the walls. In winter we have *Viburnum farreri*, followed in spring by *V. carlesii* 'Diana' and then the ancient bush of philadelphus. These three are the only survivors in this part of the earlier garden. Two *Myrtus*

Seen from the herb garden, with lavender and purple sage in the foreground, the south-east corner of the house resembles an outdoor livingroom. Sofas of upholstered box and *Salvia officinalis* 'Icterina', strewn with yellow cushions of *Euphorbia sequieriana* and *Halimium ocymoides*, stand against a retaining wall; on the carpet of lawn a box knot is filled with soft grey *Santolina neapolitana*.

communis growing in pillars against the pavilion walls provide fragrance in late summer. Terracotta pots filled with the ivy-leaved *Pelargonium* 'Amethyst' complete the scheme; in the past I have tried more ambitious combinations, but experience has proved that simplicity always seems to work best – one can have too much of a good thing!

The twin herbaceous borders were finally planted along each side of the lawn, backed by yew hedges, by then sufficiently mature to provide shelter. The planting, in every shade of white, pink and blue, provides year-round interest.

Having taken the decision to remake the whole garden and lived through the years when it looked so much worse than before, our greatest joy is to watch it become not only secret again but so much more exciting than the original.

HILARY MOGFORD, LITTLE MILTON, OXFORDSHIRE

XXII

SECRET FOR CENTURIES

'And so the garden became again an enclosed, inward-looking, secret, protected place, romantic rather than formal.'

OUR GARDEN has remained secret for hundreds of years, hidden, then as now, behind seventeenth-century houses. In an old book we found a description of the garden as it was 300 years ago, when it was much larger and served as the kitchen garden of a small abbey in the town. There was a white summerhouse with sweetbriar and *roses de Provence* growing round it; the flower and vegetable beds were edged with rosemary and had standard bay trees, brought over from Bruges. It must have been a pretty sight.

When we moved into the house in 1958, however, the garden was non-existent. What we saw was a sloping, grassy site, stripped bare of trees – all that was left after the sea had surged in one wartime night at spring-tide, when the island of Walcheren was flooded after the dykes had been bombed. The vaults and wells we struck upon while digging were the only traces of the earlier building.

For the first few years we left the garden as we had found it, being too busy restoring the big house, and working, my husband as a general practitioner and I looking after our young children. It was a perfect garden for them and their many friends, a place where they could play and romp to their hearts' content without fear of damaging anything. But, to their great indignation, times changed. My mother, a great gardener, started sending me plants from her own garden. Something had to be done with them, so I decided to put them along the edge of the lawn. And that's how the making of our garden began.

We grew more and more interested in gardening, and spent our holidays travelling about looking at other gardens. We started to make notes and consult newly acquired books, to put our latest ideas into practice, tentatively and with much trial and error. Quite often my husband would see me walking through the garden, a plant stuck on a fork, looking for a place to plant it. But, bit by bit, our plans grew more purposeful.

Creating a garden out of what we had was a real challenge. We thought it had to be in tune with the house, and over the years we made a few major decisions. First of all it had to be a garden to live in, an extension of the house. As the garden side of the house faces north-west, we looked for spots to make two terraces: one for the early morning and one for the afternoon. These terraces and the Victorian summerhouse, where we take our meals when it rains, became the focal points in our garden design.

Our next decision was to have a formal garden, using only straight lines and circles, all related to a central axis running from the middle of the sittingroom door to a chestnut tree in the middle of the lawn. All wavy lines had to be banished – quite a radical decision, but an exciting one. We discovered for ourselves how to make proportions, optical effects, illusions and equilibrium the framework of our garden.

Then came the next important decision: to level the sloping site and make small terraces, connected by steps and so creating compartments. It all made the garden appear much bigger, as did the small rectangular pool, reflecting the sky. We also

planted many hedges, some to disguise ugly views and separate the different small gardens, others with paths in between and with arches leading from one area to another. For the hedges we used yew, *Prunus laurocerasus*, privet, lonicera and espaliered apples, all pruned at various heights to give the effect of screens, like wings on a stage. And so the garden became again an enclosed, inward-looking, secret, protected place, romantic rather than formal. Although it is mainly a green garden, flowers are chosen to reflect the colours in the house. The small paved area near the house (four corner beds and a circular bed with a stone vase in the centre) is kept to white and crimson, with plants like *Sedum* 'Herbstfreude' and *Polygonum amplexicaule* 'Atrosanguineum', to match our curtains.

The garden slopes down in planted terraces to a level, rectangular lawn, edged at the far end by a symmetrical bed of yellow and white plants with touches of grey, lime-green and bronze leaves, such as *Foeniculum vulgare* 'Purpureum', which was also chosen for its strong vertical effect. At the front we put neat plants – *Alchemilla mollis, Pulmonaria officinalis* 'Sissinghurst White', large-flowered pale yellow violas, and

ABOVE: Beyond the formal roundel enclosed by clipped hedges, like wings on a stage, a secret world of light and shadow opens up. Past a patch of sunlit purple, the grass path disappears into a tunnel of intriguing darkness. RIGHT: A rose-covered arbour frames a chestnut tree set in the lawn at the heart of the garden. The cool and spring-like planting is mostly green, touched by yellow and white.

Origanum vulgare 'Aureum' – to cover the ugly stems of the taller plant growing behind them. Shrubs like *Philadelphus coronarius* 'Variegatus' and *Cornus alba* 'Sibirica' give body and form to the whole bed.

Matching borders on either side of the lawn have evenly spaced old roses and are filled with a variety of flowers in pink, crimson and all kinds of blue. Between the other plants we grow standard clematis, mainly purple and dark red, such as *Clematis viticella* 'Purpurea Plena Elegans', 'Rouge Cardinal', 'Madame Julia Correvon', 'Niobe', 'Kermesina', 'Etoile Violette', and many other varieties.

I think I love the roses best, and I always try to fit in a few more. It is a great delight to watch a newly acquired shrub coming into flower for the first time – I can hardly wait to see the first flowers on the *Rosa × centifolia* 'Batavica', chosen mainly for its name, as I was born in Batavia, now Djakarta.

The peak of our garden season is the month of June. That is the time people come to visit, sharing with us their knowledge and pleasure in plants and widening our horizons. They drive up the noisy street, ring our bell and walk through the house to be surprised by our secret garden.

JETTY DE LA HAYZE, SEISDAM, HOLLAND

XXIII

A MUCH VISITED SOLITUDE

The ice-house, masquerading as a pyramidal mortuary chapel.

L<small>E DESERT DE RETZ</small> was the archetype of the picturesque parks of the late eighteenth century in France, and today its wilderness garden, a private retreat within the wider landscape of the park, is one of the most important surviving from that period. To the visitor, its sense of history is all-pervasive. It seems only right, therefore, to allow the eloquent voices of observers from the past, contemporaries of its creator, to conjure up a vision of the garden.

A contemporary account is provided by Bachaumont in a secret memoir of 1781:

> *'Le Désert, although only twenty miles from Paris, has become the focus for excursions by amateurs, but they are only admitted by tickets issued personally by Monsieur de Monville, who never refuses them to respectable people. The property covers ninety acres surrounded by a wall – the Queen has been there several times and much enjoys it . . .'*

François de Monville had reached the mature age of forty when he undertook the transformation of his Wilderness into a Paradise Lost or Regained. It was he who decided to give his property the title of Le Désert – Retz was only added later. Like a painter in front of his canvas, he proceeded by successive brush strokes, whether in the pur-

An eighteenth-century visitor remarked on the 'immense column, looking on the outside a mere ruin, but the interior of which was done in the most refined taste . . . The most surprising feature was a beautifully designed staircase, rising in a spiral to the very top . . . On each tread there was a pot of flowers so that whether one looked up, or down, all one could see was a garland of flowers.'

chase of land, the building of follies or the creation of plantations. Originally planned as a garden of some few acres, it expanded imperceptibly over a period of ten years, from 1774 to 1785. At its peak, there were no fewer than twenty buildings in the park, many of them designed by M. de Monville himself.

Significantly, when M. de Monville commissioned a series of watercolours to publicize his newly created garden, he published them in book form with a frontispiece describing it as an 'English garden, known as Le Désert, situated in the Forest of Marly'. There speaks the wily courtier still smarting at his exclusion from Court following the succession of Louis XV, not only making believe it was by royal favour that he had been able to create his domain within that of the Crown, but also willing his visitors and readers to think he was still at Court. In fact Le Désert is on the fringe of the Forest of Marly, on land that never belonged to the King, although he did have to seek leave of his new sovereign in order to traverse the royal forest. The entrance to Le Désert was deliberately set to face the forest so that the King might find it an intriguing route to take in a break from hunting. Thus the illusion of privileged access was given to the many visitors – among them the Queen herself.

Bachaumont goes on to record that 'the most curious feature of this Thebaid today is the Chinese pavilion' – an opinion confirmed by an

The Gothic-windowed gable end wall of a church, re-erected here by the garden's creator, François de Monville. At its peak, there were no fewer than twenty buildings in the park, many of them designed by M. de Monville himself. Le Désert is the archetype of the picturesque parks of the late eighteenth century in France. Today it is one of the most important survivors from that period.

expert gardener, the Prince de Ligne, the owner of Bel Oeil. He wrote that 'the Emperor of China would acknowledge the little Chinese Pavilion of Monsieur de Monville, which is a model of research. Below it, a small spring gushes out from a large rosette, flows down in a fair stream with two small islands, and fills several basins on the terraces.'

The Prince also describes the Temple of Pan 'by a natural ravine and backing onto a wood that is visible from every side. It dominates . . . and is decorative from all points of view.'

Another acute observer, General Baron Thiebault, who visited Le Désert as a young man in 1789, later recalled in his memoirs the:

'immense column, looking on the outside a mere ruin, but the interior of which seemed to be the home of Love, of the Graces and of Fortune. Everything was indeed done in the most refined and lavish taste, but the most surprising feature was a beautifully designed staircase, rising in a spiral to the very top of this strange building. . . . On each tread there was a pot of flowers, so that whether one looked up or down the well of the staircase, where stood a charming statue of the god of love, all one could see was a garland of flowers which, constantly renewed, perfumed all the rooms.'

In this way pleasure, nature and architecture were inextricably linked at Le Désert, both outside and in the interior, where mirrors reflected infinite glimpses of the landscape framed by the windows.

The Scottish gardener Thomas Blaikie also visited Le Désert. He was employed by the Duc de Chartres at the Parc Monceau, and a certain rivalry existed between him and M. de Monville. Blaikie's tone is less than laudatory:

'the tope of the tower seemed to have been ruined. I cannot think but he meant to emitate the tower of Babel. . . . The whole of the park was a Laberynth of rather narrow crooked walks without forming many agreeable Landscapes . . .'

The other great architectural curiosity of Le Désert is the ice house, masquerading as a pyramidal mortuary chapel. Based on the antique tomb of Caius Sextus in Rome, the idea was to be copied by Thomas Jefferson, who installed one for President Madison in the basement of a Doric temple on his property at Montpelier in Virginia. Jefferson had visited Le Désert in 1786 in the company of the beautiful Maria Cosway.

Today Le Désert is a remarkable survival buried improbably within a suburb of Paris. Now a mere sixteen acres, it is gradually being restored by a society of enthusiasts set up by Jean-Marc Heftler-Louiche and myself. I became captivated by the place when I was a student, and fortunately made a survey of it when more of its buildings were extant.

The entrance to the garden is still as M. de Monville planned it, as surprising and as secret as he intended, with no hint of what lies beyond. A simple gateway of huge stone blocks opens into a natural grotto with an arch of roughly hewn rock. Through the grotto can be glimpsed M. de Monville's column-house – huge for a folly, small for a house – with its fluted exterior and raggedly ruined top.

Walking towards the column other buildings appear. To the left is the ice house, and from inside the column the Temple of Pan can be seen, and the Gothic-windowed gable end of a church removed by M. de Monville and re-erected here. But gone is the open-air theatre by the side of the path leading to the column; gone too the 'Hotthouses' admired by Blaikie. The saddest loss is the Chinese pavilion, destroyed some fifteen years ago.

M. de Monville's main motive in creating Le Désert from what Thiebault described as 'an arid and unrewarding site' was to make an intimate garden, a solitary place which by its very nature must be visited, a delightful landscape in which to receive close friends without ceremony. Born of the imagination of a man whose bedside reading was the Encyclopédie and whose financial means enabled him to satisfy his desires, Le Désert became one of the models for the Anglo-Chinese garden. It is a personal creation *par excellence*, a place where dreams are to be enjoyed. In it Utopia has become reality, its gardeners transformed into painters and philosophers.

OLIVIER CHOPPIN DE JANVRY, LE DÉSERT DE RETZ, FRANCE

XXIV

ECHOES OF CHILDHOOD

Ivy surrounds a spirit of the garden, sculpted by Simon Verity.

THE SPIRITUAL ROOTS of this garden reach back to my childhood, when an early experience helped form an inner image of what a garden should be. For a few years during the war, our family lived in Austria, in a rather neglected early eighteenth-century manor house hidden away in a small, faraway valley and surrounded by large chestnut and fir trees. It seemed absolutely remote from the horrible events of that time.

In the yard an ancient lime tree gave shade to our childhood games and on the garden side was a light parterre à l'anglais. Clean gravel paths led past areas of lawn blooming with strong roses – we could just reach their large flowers with our noses and were pleased by their heavy scent. The parterre was half-hidden under the spreading branches of an old fir tree; we felt uneasy there in the everlasting twilight, but from here the garden's secrets could be discovered. A tufa grotto served as shelter from thunderstorms; as soon as the sun came out again we fled back to the fresh air. The contrast between ordered arrangements and hidden scents, the abundance of the roses with their wasting fragrance, all this was an unforgettable part of the special attraction of our fleeting wartime garden. I have kept those feelings, memories and and images locked inside me ever since.

Many years passed before I had the chance to make a garden of my own, not in Austria but in Germany. Situated on a southern slope, the land clearly called for terraces, and so three different gardens were created. Previously you could oversee the whole area by looking down from the higher terrace at the level of the house, but now hedges and a sunken garden provide secret places for the visitor to discover.

These different rooms are more or less strictly divided from each other, connected by axes and vistas, with eye-catching objects to arouse curiosity and increase expectation. When the side doors of the summer house are open and a light breeze comes up the hill, it is the perfect place to enjoy a fresh summer morning, made fragrant by the roses and honeysuckle growing up and over it. To the left the view leads down a few steps to the rose garden with its ancient roses. In front of the summer house a long ribbon of lawn extends, striped by the strange, shifting shadows of the cut lime trees.

Looking beyond along a narrow passage through a hedge, you can glimpse the sculpture of a girl at the end of the vista. This is Daphne's kingdom – a square garden room, completely surrounded by hedges, with a roundel of lawn in the centre. On late afternoons the bench is a natural place to rest, especially charming when *Rosa* 'Sanders' White Rambler' sends its cascades down from the pergola and honeysuckle wastes its fragrance until far into the night.

When dusk falls, the scented

A purple tide sweeps through the border, paling as it rises, from rich *Geranium* x *magnificum* through mauve *Stachys macrantha* to soft lilac valerian, until it reaches the summer house, half-hidden in a cloud of white *Rosa* 'Seagull'. In early morning or late afternoon, this summer garden glows with opulent colour, its essence distilled in the perfect shape of the purple globe at the heart of the border.

167370

petals of the evening primroses unfold in the sunken garden, their full yellow bowls shining long in the darkness while the silvery-grey of wormwood and cotton lavender is slowly extinguished. If you make your way down to the Purple Garden, the pink *damascena* rose 'Celsiana' on either side of the steps enchants you as you pass by. From everywhere in the garden you are surrounded by wonderful fragrances.

In summer this garden also enjoys a festival of colour. The Purple Garden profits from the rich hue and large flowers of *Geranium* x *magnificum*, floating in clouds of deep indigo, joined later by *G. pratense* and *G. psilostemon*. Other, taller plants in varying shades of purple intensify the game of colours, which culminates in June.

Below a slope the main border is framed by the Rambler roses 'Veilchenblau' and 'Amethyst'. The lay-out of this area, slightly terraced and stepped, is also symmetrical, so that the effect of the colours is heightened. As you stroll by, the central perspective changes to a diagonal one and the holy order of symmetry falls into happy chaos. Early in the morning and

PREVIOUS PAGE: A bench naturalized by *Hydrangea macrophylla* and the strong leaves of *H. quercifolia* 'Snow Queen'. *H. M.* 'Blaumeise' stand in pots beside the bench; in the evening the narcotic scent of lonicera fills this small enclosure. ABOVE: A sundial in the sunken garden, overhung with 'Rose de Rescht'. The tall yellow heads of *Sisyrinchium striatum* echo the grey spikes of stachys.

from late afternoon, reds and blues predominate; as dusk starts to fall, these begin to gleam and when darkness has finally swallowed the green of the foliage, they appear to take wing and drift on the air.

Scent and colour impress the visitor, but so does the incidence of abundance and order. Even in winter the garden is not without charm, more transparent than in summer and with evergreens – hedges, yew and box topiary – playing their part. Suddenly, when snow falls, the atmosphere changes. Never is the garden stranger than at this time. Stiff and lifeless, it seems created for its own sake, with no human origins, imbued with a solemn calm that the gardener hesitates to disturb; the line of his footprints on the lawn leaves an impertinent trace on the immaculate whiteness. But it is a fleeting moment before the spell is broken, and the melting snow begins to drip from the bushes and the green lawn shines through even more vividly. A few remnants of snow lie on the grass to remind us of winter's brief span, but here and there burgundy-coloured Lent roses are already greeting the garden as early messengers of spring.

REINER HERLING, DORTMUND, GERMANY

XXV

BEHIND EARTH WALLS

The garden is enclosed by 'Knicks', earth walls planted with trees and shrubs, which have stamped their character on the face of this region. They served at once as protection against wind and strangers, as markers of estate boundaries and enclosures for the peasants' cattle. Today these roles no longer apply, but these "Knicks" will continue to be preserved, as a refuge for flora and fauna . . .'

OFF THE ROAD along which the hereditary dukes of Oldenburg once travelled to their pleasance at the Castle of Rastede, a farmhouse was built at the turn of the century. Man and beast sheltered together under its deep-eaved roof. The farmhouse and its outbuildings were surrounded by oak trees offering protection from the strong west winds, firewood for the winter and acorns for the pigs in autumn. Traditionally, on the birth of a daughter, the farmer would select the best trees for felling to make furniture for her future bridal home.

Following the farmer's premature death, the estate was leased for decades; in 1979, it was put up for sale. As passionate gardeners, we saw a unique opportunity to create a large, highly personal garden. Casting aside the warnings of relations and friends, we bought the two-hectare property, which consisted solely of grazing land, potato fields and some buildings in a wretched state of repair – and not so much as a hint of a garden.

Today, after fifteen years of hard work and much trial and error, we do not regret our decision for an instant. We have restored the house, planted a big, big garden – or rather gardens – around it, and still have space to carry out further plans.

Join us on our tour. The garden is enclosed by 'Knicks', earth walls planted with trees and shrubs, which have stamped their character on the face of this region. They served at once as protection against wind and strangers, as markers of estate boundaries and enclosures for the peasants' cattle. Today these roles no longer apply, but these 'Knicks' will

continue to be preserved, as a refuge for flora and fauna and for the part they play in nature conservation.

From the road a wide gateway in one of the 'Knicks' leads into our garden. It is always open to friends and visitors. You will find yourself at the start of an avenue leading to an open space in front of the main entrance to the house. On the left is a line of evergreen oaks, over a hundred years old, and on the right a line of various deciduous trees which we planted to take away some of the gloom of a pure oak avenue. Our neighbours' cows still graze on the extensive pastureland to the right of the *allée*, but my husband, who laid out the whole garden, plans to transform this field into another garden, with a rhododendron *allée*, arboretum and a lawn flanked by yews.

At the end of the field, just in front of the old barn, which is still in need of repair, a path veers right to the woodland garden. To the existing old oaks we added birch and picea, many of which succumbed to the hurricane of February 1990. In retrospect, however, this was an advantage, as in our first flush of enthusiasm we planted too many trees too close together. Now the light slanting through the canopy perfectly meets the needs of the shrubs and rhododendrons planted beneath them.

Here, near the large curving borders of shrubs, chosen for the colour of their flowers and foliage, we have planted, with the help of a specialist nurseryman, a collection of rare hostas. A host of different hellebores ensure that this part of the garden is interesting at times of the year when flowers are scarce.

Enclosed by earth ramparts, known locally as 'Knicks'
– a regional tradition – the garden is inward-looking;
each little enclosure has its own character. Here a
white-painted bench sits in an arbour of clipped beech,
offering a carefully stage-managed view of the pool
beyond. Water-lilies float on its surface and, around
the edge, purple-flowered iris have colonized.

The remaining birch trees, which make up a small grove, are underplanted with early-flowering plants; at the start of the year the ground is transformed into a bright-coloured carpet. We pass the place where the deer come to drink and carry on along the 'bear track', lined with sculptures created by my husband, to a lawn fringed with oaks, where a circular stone-paved sitting area has a barbecue in the centre.

From here our tour leads towards the rear of the house and the enclosed formal garden furnished with traditional cottage garden plants – delphiniums, phlox, gypsophila, chrysanthemums, coreopsis and poppies, including one of my favourites, *Papaver orientale* 'Grave Witwe', which I saw first in the famous garden of the painter Emil Nolde in Niebüll. The nearby vegetable garden is protected by a drystone wall with herbs for the kitchen planted at its base.

Your eye will now be caught by a small alpine bed planted with a variety of large-rosetted, bright-coloured sempervirens and delicate saxifrages, fritillaries and iris. The climate of north-west Germany does not favour them and they tend to damp off, but with persistence we have managed to make them thrive here.

In the rose garden Hybrid Teas predominate. Between them old apple trees, which scarcely bear fruit now and really belong on the bonfire, have found a new role as supports for climbing roses and clematis, displaying their beauty much more naturally than man-made frames. On the gable side of the house a bed is laid out with miniature roses, which benefit from the shelter given by the house from the wind and glare of the sun. Here and there box balls lie as if scattered at random.

We leave the rose garden by a path set between a pair of herbaceous borders with parallel plantings of many kinds of peony, including my cherished 'Chocolate Soldier' with its deep red blooms. Old hybrid rhododendrons form a protective backcloth, and between them, as if they had been rolled out from the rose garden, are more box balls.

On the right-hand side we pass a bed with yellow-leaved shrubs such as *Symphytum* 'Goldsmith' and a golden hebe from England, and on the left-hand side a collection of rarities, among them a huge *Cardiocrinum giganteum*, extremely unusual here. We are aiming now for the old rose garden – almost fifty varieties, some trained over arbours. Here too is the Alba rose, which, when we took over the estate, was the only garden plant. Further on we come across *R*. 'Agnes', which I brought from my great-grandmother's house; for me its scent is redolent of the perfume of all old roses, and its golden foliage is especially decorative in autumn.

A complete contrast is the marshy bed on the left, where orchids have colonized in front of the water-lily pool. The white bench in the beech bower is a perfect spot to view the pool and the lawn towards the house.

Now we are being drawn in a great arc back to the house, past the autumn beds with shrubs and grasses, planted especially for their late flowers and attractive autumn colours. The large drifts of narcissus, primulas and tulips disappear after they have flowered into the leafy masses of the hostas and thence to the magnificent yellow-flowered plants – hemerocallis, *Iris sibirica* 'Butter and Sugar' and *Rudbeckia fulgida* var. *sullivantii* 'Goldsturm'.

This path ends in the entrance walk leading to the opening between the house and the farm buildings. In its centre is a fine example of *Cercidiphyllum japonicum*. If you stand here in the autumn, you cannot be sure whether the scent comes from this tree or from the hospitable kitchen, where refreshment is being prepared for our visitors, so that they can see and admire everything that has not been mentioned in this account of our garden.

WOLFGANG AND HILLE HAUCKE, RASTEDE, GERMANY

XXVI

THE CAMELLIA GARDEN

'Casa do Campo . . . is a fascinating example of an architectural topiary garden. The enormous size of the clipped shapes, studded in spring with brilliant, delicate flowers in shades of white, rose and red, make it a place of hidden delight as well as a horticultural curiosity.'

CAMELLIAS ARE so widely cultivated in the north of Portugal that the shrubs often serve to line the streets, while on festive occasions the flowers are massed to form carpets of colour. Even more dramatically, they are used in this part of the country as the basic plant in topiary.

The art of modelling trees by trimming and forcing them to grow in predetermined shapes and directions has been practised at least since the first century. Originally the creations were bizarre and fantastic, but from the fifteenth century they became more regular and architectural – hedges, arches, tunnels and even pavilions of clipped foliage entered the vocabulary of the garden. Portuguese topiary is of this type; some of the examples in the north of the country date from the end of the eighteenth century.

The topiary shapes may be conventional, but the use of camellias is innovative and unusual. Tradition has it that a seventeenth-century sailor brought some plants back with him from Japan to a garden near Oporto, from where it was introduced into the garden of Casa do Campo. One camellia tree surviving here is perhaps the oldest in Europe. Soon after its introduction into Portugal a method was perfected of saving the flower buds when pruning the foliage, so that the topiary would then carry a mosaic of eye-catching rose-coloured camellia flowers the following spring.

Casa do Campo, spread out against a background of wooded hills in the valley of the Tamega, is a fascinating example of an architectural topiary garden. The enormous size of the clipped shapes, studded in spring with brilliant, delicate flowers in shades of white, rose and red, make it a place of hidden delight as well as a horticultural curiosity.

The house has always belonged to my family. Although containing decorative elements of the sixteenth century, it dates mainly from the seventeenth century; its enlargement through the years has resulted in a picturesque composition. The neighbouring church, the entrance terrace and the garden stand at different angles to each other, and this irregular juxtaposition is softened by rich plantings of hortensia, lonicera and agapanthus. The baroque façade of the church is exactly matched botanically by the pair of araucarias from Queensland, *A. bidwillii*, which frame it.

The setting of the garden in relation to the house is also unusual: access is a bridge at first-floor level. This guarantees privacy but makes it impossible for the whole of the garden to be seen. It was to compensate for this that topiary was chosen, its columns and peaks visible not only from the house but also from the terrace, where today the huge clipped shapes tower menacingly, as if they were gigantic green monsters just settled on this peaceful landscape.

An architectural topiary garden carved out of camellias is hard to imagine. Yet here in northern Portugal is just such a garden, with a series of outdoor rooms enclosed by glossy dark camellia foliage which in spring bursts into bloom with thousands of ornamental flowers. Many of the specimens are a century old and more – one is reputed to be a survivor from the seventeenth century.

Looking from the house across the concealed swimming pool, a veritable townscape of camellias comes into view. Clipped by the imaginative hand of its creator into domes, spirals and turrets, it has been maintained by his painstaking successors. If you venture into the archway, you find yourself in the enclosed central room of the tunnel of camellias shown in the previous photograph.

Once in the garden these fantastic effects disappear and an orderly parterre opens up, with eight flower beds grouped round a central fountain. The large scale of the beds is complemented by the double box hedge which encloses them. Camellia topiary still dominates, however, especially in and beyond the sequence of green rooms extending along the main axis of the garden.

The central room, the only one to be completely covered, is circular, reflecting the round water tank in the middle. Doors and windows have been opened in the surrounding hedges, reinforcing the architectural character. The other rooms also have camellia walls and steeply sloping 'roofs'. Tall cylinders, rings, umbrellas, arches and domes complete the rich range of shapes which make this a garden of fanciful artistry.

ANTONIO LEIDT, CECORICO DE BASTO, PORTUGAL

XXVII

NATURE IN ITS PERFECT STATE

Hewn from a single block of stone, a lantern in the pool.

FOR AS LONG as I can remember, I have been fascinated by the art and culture of eastern Asia. When, twenty years ago, we were planning our house and our plot of land, my immediate thought was that the garden must have at least a touch of Japan.

The more I studied this distant culture, the more its secret nature appealed to me. The gardens there have an intensity, a distillation of thought, which speaks directly to our souls. The ultimate goal is to experience nature in its perfect state, and to represent Paradise – a landscape in which men live in a blissful state of harmony.

The crane and the turtle are to be found in the Chinese paradise legends as symbols of long life and health. In garden art they are suggested by a variety of different shapes. The turtle, squat and earth-bound, is represented by a group of flat rocks and rounded bushes; the crane, upright and graceful, as oddly cropped pines or vertical compositions in stone. The juxtaposition of rough rock against soft moss, or the umbrella-like forms of the pines against the cushion shape of clipped azaleas, is an essential part of Japanese garden art. It becomes a harmonious game, relying, as in painting, on the flow of lines, colours and shapes. Movement, represented by the judicious placing of plants, stones, mounds and paths, plays an essential part in this game.

It is not satisfactory to lay out a garden in a technically correct manner – it should have a personal radiation, releasing a feeling of peace, well-being and absolute harmony in the spectator, who will be completely enchanted by the garden.

We have terraced our garden on three different levels, dividing the areas into several rooms by means of planting and groups of stones. The parts of the garden which seem to be furthest away are those which are lower than the others. Clipped box balls and semi-circular yew hedges merge into each other creating the impression of a hilly landscape. Rocks and plants with rounded sides and flat tops convey a feeling of symmetry and harmony. The habit of growth of the umbrella pines is controlled by clipping, as is the size of the rhododendrons and azaleas, so that the proportions of the garden do not change much over time.

The relationship in shape and colour between house, stones, pool and plants has also been considered with care in order to achieve a harmony of forms and colours. The paths are laid out to lead visitors on to new viewpoints, inviting them to stay and absorb the atmosphere of each room; they converge on a resting point, a terrace on the hill, where they can look over the pool and all the other different levels.

The front of the house has a roofed wooden walk leading out onto a square terrace raised on supports. The house is just an extension of the garden – its own rooms are oriented towards the garden and filled with glass, so that we always feel close to nature as we watch the water of the pool reflecting the heavens, enjoy the goldfish playing, the iridescent dragonflies and the frogs sunning themselves on the water-lily leaves, and listen to the music of the waterfalls.

Pink water-lilies and orange day-lilies seen against a backcloth of boulders and green foliage of all shapes and textures are reflected in the still waters of the pool. Rounded rocks and bushes – symbols of the turtle in Chinese paradise legends – are an integral part of the garden's character, which has evolved from a lifetime's fascination with the art and culture of eastern Asia.

The creation of my garden has been linked with my thoughts of dreams, fairytales and tenderness. Just as I paint my pictures in soft, muted tones, so I have fashioned my garden like a delicate watercolour painting, with fine and pale flowers beside soft green foliage in contrast to the dark green of the pines.

Above all, the garden is where we experience the seasons and the cyclical power of nature. Spring is soft and serene, the atmosphere created by the full flowering of the rhododendrons and azaleas in shades ranging from white to rose and strong pink, violet to pale yellow. They are placed so that no plant diminishes the impact of any other. The whole garden is kept to these muted shades apart from a small area at the end of the terrace, where *Azalea pontica* hybrids change to yellow, orange and red, increasing in intensity to a flaming inferno which reflects itself in the pool.

In summer the garden is clothed in shades of green – deep dark Austrian pine, light ferns, fresh moss, soft box balls, and back to the dark foliage of the many different rhododendrons which serve as a background. The large proportion of evergreen trees and shrubs means that the garden makes an impact even in the winter months when other gardens tend to look bare and empty.

There are also some favourite decorative plants demanding our notice. The early-flowering cherries, *Prunus* × *subhirtella* 'Autumnalis', are followed by the camellias. In the middle of April, *Prunus* 'Kiku-shidare-zakura', wrapped in its rose-coloured dress, dominates the whole picture from the island in the pond. At the end of the month the first rhododendrons come into bloom, the *R. williamsianum* hybrids with their bewitching flowers and delicate scent. These are followed by the *R. yakushimanum* hybrids and their wild varieties, which I treasure most of all.

The Japanese azaleas, *A. pontica*, and a multitude of different rhododendrons flower in the middle of May, when *Cornus kousa* 'Madame Butterfly' displays its large green-white blooms – they really do resemble butterflies. Then it is the turn of the soft-coloured *Paeonia suffruticosa* to make its appearance. In my garden this time in May is the high point, when I feel as if I were in Paradise. Best are the early morning hours: the cool of the night and the humidity coming from the wood have refreshed the flowers during the spell of darkness; then, as the sun starts to slant through the trees onto the soft flowers of azaleas and rhododendrons, the light softens them even more. Then I'm keen to breathe in the scent of the flowers, listen to the voices of the birds and the splashing of the water, and notice the singing of the wind. The mood is dependent on the changing light during the day. Filled with joy, you are aware of the importance of each and every life.

At the beginning of June, *Kalmia latifolia* blooms in many different shades, and the water-lily flowers appear, some luxuriant forms lasting until the autumn. As the month draws to a close, the hemerocallis show their gratitude by bringing forth new flowers each day. Meconopsis, with its unbelievable heavenly blue flowers, grows man-high and tolerates no competition from its neighbours.

During the warm months of July and August the garden is wrapped in a fresh peaceful green. Retreating from the frenzy of the town and our business life, we are overcome by a feeling of serenity as we step through the terrace door into an enchanted world which feeds our souls and enables us to enjoy the pleasures of life.

RENATE RICHI, SYDIKUM, GERMANY

XXVIII

RICHES IN A LITTLE ROOM

'*Seven miles north of Maastricht's ancient fortifications is an English garden, enriched by and in harmony with its alien surroundings.*'

A LITTLE WAY above the village of Rekem, the river changes name – from Meuse to Maas – and character. From its distant source in Haute-Marne, 200 miles away, on a hillside exactly due south, the Meuse has traced its course and history around granite spurs, through wooded glens, past ancient battles, to Mosa Trajectum, the ford across the Maas. Admired by the Roman settlers for its gentle climate where maritime and continental air masses meet, the valley has widened now to an orchard strath. From here, north and west to the sea, the bountiful land astride the river gradually changes its appearance as it merges into Holland.

The Maas shaped the landscape, the communications and the economy. Its valley crafted gardens for the emperor Charlemagne, worshippping at the Cathedral, building a small palace nearby. It brought the Norsemen inland, built the region's early wealth with taxes on the great Flemish wool trade passing through to Cologne on the Rhine, and nurtured the evolution of an indigenous art which inspired medieval miniaturists, painters and sculptors in wood. Steeped in strife (the history of the Low Countries is really a chronicle of Maasland wars), the tranquillity of the years between the conflicts has now returned.

Near the water, seven miles north of Maastricht's ancient fortifications, is an English garden, enriched by and in tune with its alien surroundings.

Standing in the wings of the rose garden gives a tantalizing glimpse of the set-piece stage beyond. A clipped topiary figure occupies centre stage, with *Rosa* 'Raubritter' spotlit from the left. *R. rubrifolia* cascades down the clipped hedge and 'Village Maid' and 'White Wings', hover in the background, where iron standards support various clematis. Nepeta spills out over the mellow brick paving.

No garden can be static. The generations pass and new ideas prompt development or rejection. But amid the fluidity of an annually regenerating garden the sense of continuity is soothing and unchanging. Old trees express this well, as the soft pastel colours of their trunks blend into borders against old brick walls. The Maasland was once an oak forest, but in this garden beech, lime, spruce and other trees predominate, sheltering and screening the shrubs. Three great golden elms, traditional coffin wood, hint at mortality and eternal rest.

The tall house is on the north side, leaving the garden open to the sun throughout the day, shaded only by trees, hedges and high walls. The area is rich in songbirds and butterflies. *Multum in parvo*: here there is indeed much in little, for the grounds extend to less than a quarter of a hectare. When I started the design thirty years ago I knew I would have to compress without crowding, balancing the lawns with high-density planting, if I were to achieve the variety I sought in an all-season garden. This restriction has inevitably influenced my choice, but I do not think it has in any way impoverished it.

I was fortunate in my inheritance of a remarkable gazebo – huge in size and made of *Cornus mas* – which, seen easily from the house, forms a natural focus of attention, leading the viewer into the garden and setting the mood. Apart from this ancient piece of living architecture,

I was unable to use monumental size in anything, so I relied heavily on shape to enhance the vertical geometry, continuing the influence of the gazebo into the topiary clipping, although a pair of taxodiums, a koelreuteria and a ginkgo, together with the elms, do raise the eyes.

The garden relies very much on classical disciplines. Underlying the occasional use of colour in the borders are the recollected virtues of simplicity, the symmetrical balance of the lawns governing the metre. The rhythm reflects the pervasive glamour of green – homeopathic, subtle to the senses, soothing to the eye, cool in the heat. Wherever the tints are close-packed and intense, there are reminders of infinite riches in a little room, but their logic is perceptible and not dull. The contrasts are designed to exploit the region's hospitable climate and generous fertility with their hues and dimensions, textures and scents and proportions.

The garden has an end piece, an archaic and formal tribute to the Maasland heritage. The visitor has been drawn on, scanning quickly in anticipation of a leisurely wander along a retraced path. Suddenly the progress halts. The fruit garden

The smallness of the pool is highlighted by the scale and wealth of the layered planting surrounding it. Hostas glow blue against the massive clipped hedge, its gentle curve emphasized by the bower of Rosa 'Kathleen' and the standard honeysuckles in front. The geometry of the pool is marked by box balls, which in turn are lightened by a sprinkling of alchemilla, ferns and Welsh poppies.

was the earliest cultivation of our ancestors, and here is another, barely five years old. Hidden by mature brick walls and a high taxus hedge and only 13 by 7 metres in size, this orchard has fifty espaliered apple trees and pear trees, their future size and form still merely hinted at. Their symmetrical distribution is shaped by a maze of miniature box hedges, but the variety of their fruit and colour, the contrast of their many different shapes and sizes and the promise of their mellow future never fail to intrigue me.

Beneath the trees a carpet of herbs, lavender, iris and strawberries are a feast to the eye. In spring drifts of blue *Scilla siberica* and fritillaries are followed by green and white striped Viridiflora tulips, and in summer white and cream roses prolong the blossom's tints. A little later many different varieties of small-flowered clematis, *C. alpina*, *C. macropetala* and especially *C. viticella*, weave their way through the laden branches amid the ripening fruit. True to their inheritance, the colours are soft and gentle, delicately counterpointing the vivid borders outside. Here is the culmination and the quintessence of the valley of the Maas.

PATRICIA VAN ROOSMALEN, REKEM, BELGIUM

XIX

A GARDEN IN A FOREST GLADE

A stone bust gains a hat and tippet of purest white ermine.

I FELL IN LOVE with Walenburg when it was a ruin and I was a bride-to-be. 'If you marry me, we'll live there,' my fiancé promised. And so we do, although it was a longish wait of twenty-three years before we moved in.

Miraculously meanwhile our tenants, Mr and Mrs Canneman, had built this most secret of Dutch gardens, which is now administered by the Nederlandse Tuinenstichting. If you drive too fast along the ditch-lined road out of the village of Langbroek you will miss it completely, and even if you spot the entrance by the thirteenth-century tower of the house, you will still not guess that hidden behind hedges of hornbeam and yew is an acre of the Netherlands that is a tribute to the genius of Sissinghurst – its roundel and its rooms – a concept unfamiliar in Holland when the Cannemans started the garden in 1965.

I love the secrecy of these rooms, all the more because they are set in our Dutch meadows, romantically sheltered by 150-year-old oaks and shallow moats on all sides. These moats are our secret weapon against rabbits and roedeer, effective lifesavers for plants in all but the most icy of winters, when they freeze over and we have to shoot the rabbits from the top of the tower. We can chase the roedeer but the harm is done overnight and many plants are eaten.

Thirty years ago this was a wilderness, impossible to garden because of the dreaded blue clay, whose deadly effect was intensified by heavy rainfall and long winters. The original plan was for yew hedges everywhere, but after two abortive attempts this was modified to part taxus and part hornbeam (*Carpinus betulus*). Now that the hedges are mature I'm glad of that – on such a small scale yew everywhere would have been very oppressive. As it is, the four rooms are so sheltered and secret that my husband need never fear detection as he sips the little tipple he keeps hidden in the *Rosa* 'Viridiflora' in the rose garden. . . . It's hard to believe that the blue clay in that spot was 1.3 metres deep in places and said by local wisdom to be undiggable.

Every room has its own charm but in June this particular rose garden is our favourite. The dead-heading is quite a job, which is mostly done early in the morning. You can always see how the atmosphere of this garden affects people when they enter it. They fall silent as if in church.

One of the mysterious sides to owning a garden is that you look at plants and always remember their history. After twenty-five years these roses, having set their roots firmly in the clay, are still thriving, but their beginnings here were dramatic: they all were ordered specially from England but were promptly put into quarantine and thus missed the planned November planting.

Other roses, particularly the ramblers twining over the hornbeam hedges, have grown far beyond what the Cannemans can have imagined. Just outside the hedges of the 'quiet' or 'white' garden, 'Kiftsgate' and 'Cerise Bouquet' roses rampage over the three ancient pear trees that are the sole survivors from pre-Canneman days.

Just beyond the boundaries are other treasurs: *Ginkgo biloba, Malus toringo* (syn. *M. sieboldii*), *Pyrus salicifolia* 'Pendula', an aralia, a *Parrotia persica* which has only bloomed once in five years. At the water's edge on the southern side, the mice used to devour the many hellebores at the base of a bust of Apollo until our master cat Jan came to the rescue of the hellebores, not the mice!

There is a special satisfaction in recognizing the simplicity of some of the plantings and in appreciating how effective they are – four golden elms with self sown forget-me-nots at their feet and a circle of *Alchemilla mollis* in the centre, or a stone bench with a large hydrangea at each end set in an arch

ABOVE: Surrounded on all sides by water and protected by a dense screen of ancient oaks, the fairytale castle of Walenburg is set in an enchanted garden. LEFT: Its spacious outdoor rooms are filled to overflowing with roses, herbaceous flowers, golden foliage. The strong bones of its architectural framework, evident in winter, are all but obliterated in the summer by the abundance and richness of the planting.

of hornbeams and 'Constance Spry' roses. New aspects of the garden emerge through the seasons when seen from inside the house, a side that's perhaps difficult for garden visitors to imagine. The prunus (name unknown), for example, comes to life when seen in the distance over the violet of the rhododendron planted right up against the house; the evergreen of the osmanthus and its little white flowers, glimpsed through a window, throw a distant taxus into relief. The intertwined *Akebia quinata* and wisteria cover the house magnificently but also completely obliterate the lightning conductor – maybe it would be poetic justice if one day these botanical miracles engulfed us all completely.

COUNTESS VAN LYNDEN VAN SANDENBURG, WALENBURG, HOLLAND

XXX

IN THE HILLS OF CONNECTICUT

The scent of honeysuckle and roses wafts over a path.

THOUGH I HAVE loved nature since my early childhood, I never thought (perhaps because I have always lived in cities) that one day I would have a garden of my own. Still today, though I try very hard to learn the proper name of every plant, when someone asks me, 'What is that?' I always forget the name of even the most common of flowers in a moment of panic. Then again, I don't think that there is such a thing as a common flower, because every one is a gift from God to us.

I have lived in New York since 1963 and in the late 1960s I spent many weekends with Tatiana and Alexander Lieberman. Through them I discovered the beauty of the gently hilled part of north-west Connecticut. For the first time, I felt the urge to have something of my own in the countryside.

Brook Hill Farm was love at first sight. The house itself lies one-third of a mile along a driveway from a not very populated country lane and as I drove up – without seeing the house – I knew this was the place I wanted to be. The price, that is another story. Though I bought the house for very little money, I could not afford even the first $10 of it, but then throughout my life I have never let common sense or reason interfere with passion or with falling in love.

There was nothing particular about the house. In fact, though I think it is beautiful, Annette, my wife, thinks that it is one of the ugliest houses she has ever seen. We

One of the four main borders where colours are carefully controlled to create harmonious themes. Here the emphasis is on mauves, blues, pinks and white. A dwarf hedge can barely contain the effusion of perilla, salvia, perovskia, penstemon and scabious escaping towards the patterned brick path. The border is given extra height by the elegant trellissed tripod clothed with roses – a significant feature of the garden.

all know that love is blind. What is important about Brook Hill Farm is not the house, but the setting. The house sits on the top of a hill called Skiff Mountain and the great beauty of it is the extraordinary views. I love to walk at night when everything is dark and be able to look for miles all around without ever seeing an electric light.

The house was built in 1935 and there have been two previous owners and probably because of the natural physical beauty of the place, no one before me felt the need for a garden. In fact, many years ago when I started thinking of making a garden, I invited Russell Page to come and visit for a weekend in the hopes that he would give me some ideas of what I should do with the place. I took him on a visit and when we finally came to the terrace of the house, I was totally dismayed when he asked me, 'What is it you want to have?' 'A garden,' I replied. 'You will never have a garden,' he said. In total shock I asked why. 'You will never have a garden because a garden is a room and to have a room you need walls and you have no walls. The eyes stop at the horizon; the only thing you could do is to add more trees to frame the view.' He went on to make a plan for me which I followed completely, except for the rounded terrace in front of the house that he immediately wanted to take out. It took me twenty years to realize he was right.

Four symmetrical beds, bisected by brick paths laid in
a herringbone pattern, overflow in June with a mixture
of hardy perennials and annuals. Despite the formality
of the framework, the garden exhibits all the freedom
of a cottage garden, but the plants have been chosen
with consummate skill. The use of box as backcloth
and edging is a masterly stroke of harmony.

Russell Page was an extraordinary man. Today, when I look back, I think that it was quite daring of me to have him come when I myself knew so little about what I could do with the place. A few weeks before his visit, I had bought a gardening book from the White Flower Farm and had been working on preparing and planting a herbaceous border in a half-moon shape, about twenty feet long by six feet wide. I worked very hard on clearing and preparing the ground and on planting, following the suggested plans in the book. I was all excited in anticipation of Russell's reaction when he walked by it. In the most polite, but icy manner, he looked at it as we passed by it and asked, 'What is that?' I was so utterly embarrassed that I never told him the truth. I said that it was there when I bought the house, probably done by the previous owner and since I hadn't decided what to do with that space yet, I had left it. From that visit it has stuck in my mind that I had no rooms because I had no walls. Since then I have built nothing but walls.

It's funny how hard one works arranging a garden (now especially, with Annette's two Norfolk Terriers, Jupiter and Lily, digging full-time) for the arrival of a visitor when, in fact, I am always apprehensive that people will hate it though there is always a lot of pride in showing something one loves.

When I bought the property there was a not very attractive, recently-built horse barn on the southeast side of the house. The very first planting I ever did was a series of trees and flowering shrubs with the double purpose of starting to 'frame' the view and hide the barn from the house. If I had been brave enough or had enough money, I should have taken it out altogether. Instead, I built a swimming pool on the side of the barn, which I slowly turned into a pool house. I say slowly because at first I thought I could have the pool, the barn, and three horses. But then I realized that they were not compatible and I sacrificed having horses and put all my efforts into making a garden. Because the law requires me to fence my pool, I put a stockade fence around it but because the fence was in such an open space, from any angle it always looked liked Fort Apache. So, eventually I took the fence down and instead planted a wall of yews; this eventually became my very first 'room' where I have only white flowers of late bloom so that the garden is in flower at the time when the pool is being used.

The second room I built was in what used to be a parking area which was the access to the barn. The third room – and today my favorite one – is what I today call my 'secret garden' and which originally was intended as a rose garden. It was built in a space 50 feet by 50 feet and simply divided into four identical square planting areas by a brick path.

I have always loved roses. I think that they are one of the most satisfying flowers to grow because of their many varieties and all the purposes they serve and then the fact that most roses are fragrant, fragrance being to me the magic of a flower. I first started mainly with a garden of Hybrid Tea roses, most of them of the Peace family and always in light shades of pastel or white. Every year I would lose a tremendous amount of them, Kent being in a zone four area with temperatures sometimes dipping to twenty below zero in the winter and soaring to over a hundred at times in the summer. Though a friend gave me the advice to consider roses just as annuals, I was too heartbroken at the loss to replace most of them every year. So I decided to leave in that space all the roses that were really happy to be there (mostly climbers and old-fashioneds) and do something else.

This is the time when I first met Caroline Burgess. In the late spring of 1992, my wife and I went to visit Stonecrop, the beautiful garden of Anne and Frank Cabot near the Hudson River in Cold Springs, New York; Caroline was its director. Annette has a much better eye and far more experience in gardens than I; she always criticized my exuberant use of colors in plantings, referring to them as my 'Latino gardens'. In time I have learned from her to be much more selective in my color choices. Stonecrop consists of a series of gardens within a garden: woodlands and water, a grass garden, a Mediterranean dry garden, rock ledges, alpines and an enclosed flower garden. Besides the wonderful alpines, I was really impressed by the beauty, charm and creativity of Stonecrop's walled flower garden.

I was so utterly taken by it that I visited the garden a second time, this time taking with me my two caretakers, Roger Whitmore and Felix Trinidad, so that they could themselves see the beauty of the garden and how well it was tended. I was taken by the notion of creating something in this spirit in my space. So I decided to call Caroline and ask her if it would amuse her – and if she had any extra time apart from her many

duties at Stonecrop – to help me plan the garden on a freelance basis. I think she was totally taken aback by my request, but when I get something in my mind, I won't give up and I kept calling her until I finally persuaded her to come here to Connecticut and look at the space.

So, early this spring, we started working in the garden and although 75 per cent of the planting is done with perennials and the rest with annuals and biennials, it's amazing that the garden today looks as if it has always been there. I would say that there are between fifteen and twenty plants (sometimes of the same variety, sometimes a mixture) in the space where other gardeners might have put only one. But the effect is breathtakingly beautiful. I don't want to sound conceited in saying so but I think I can say it because it's not my creation alone. In a way, not only do I think of this as Caroline's garden, but also as a little bit of Rosemary Verey's garden, as

LEFT AND ABOVE: Following Russell Page's advice when he found Brook Hill Farm set on an exposed hillside, the owner created walls for protection and designed rooms within them. His third room was originally intended as a rose garden, divided into four square planting areas. It became his most secret garden, furnished with the sensitivity and unerring skill of the fashion designer.

Caroline started her gardening life with her at Barnsley in England.

A garden is probably the most spiritual and pure of joys that one is ever likely to encounter. It's a communion with nature and beauty in the most simple and fundamental form – to be appreciated and understood it is an experience that should be *lived* at every instant.

In a garden, one cannot reflect on something bad, but only think of positive things. At the same time, what is truly wonderful about a garden is that it teaches you a lesson about life's continuity. The reason why there are such wonderful gardens all over the world is that people have had the wisdom to plant a tree knowing that they may never see the tree in its prime, but that other future generations will. In a sense, a garden is a fragile vision that can quickly disappear out of neglect, but with constant work and tender love it can preserve beauty forever.

OSCAR DE LA RENTA, BROOK HILL FARM, CONNECTICUT

EXUBERANT GARDENS

The flower-beds all were liberal of delight;
Roses in heaps were there, both red and white,
Lilies angelical, and gorgeous glooms
Of wall-flowers, and blue hyacinths, and blooms
Hanging thick clusters from light boughs; in short,
All the sweet cups to which the bees resort.
With plots of grass, and leafier walks between
Of red geraniums, and of jessamine . . .

Leigh Hunt (1784–1859): from *The Story of Rimini*

XXXI

GARDEN SECRETS

Rhododendron 'Rose Bud' is reflected in the water-lily pond.

SECRET GARDENS – garden secrets: does the gardener carry them deep in his mind or are they born from the very earth? Or is there perhaps some secret bond between them?

I believe there is a kind of symbiosis between a gardener and his garden, born of careful watchfulness, or marvelling, of toil and love.

A garden is a living being which cannot exist without continuing exchanges. A garden receives as also it gives. Like a mirror it is a reflection of its creator, but it also pursues its own life in the fullness of its passionate saps. Its exuberance evokes a river spilling over the surrounding fields – but this wandering water holds the entire sky.

My secret gardens were born one by one over the years, since that day in 1976 when I first looked upon this small piece of the world which was to change my life.

There, lying between two old walls, was a longish, abandoned stretch of grass with a clump of lilacs and an abundance of nettles. At the back two large trees framed within their branches a distant hill on which the crop fields drew oblique lines of brown and green up to the horizon; a wood grew all along the undulating ridge. Beyond my cheerless domain I received this landscape created by nature as a gift and a hope . . . and so I set purposefully to work.

The land I owned was dismally flat and I decided to transform it into

Stormy April skies and the long shadows of bare branches and clipped hedges give a theatrical setting to the springtime gentleness of this, the oldest part of the garden. *Exochorda* x *macrantha* 'The Bride' spreads its white dress beneath a towering *Prunus* 'Amanogawa'. Spring flowers compete with the new leaves, and over the first foliage-covered arch the fields of Normandy are seen in the distance.

'chambers' so that each step might bring a surprise, a discovery, a difference in shapes and colours. Close to the house, where blues and pinks predominate, I made a point of always mixing evergreen shrubs for winter days with spring and summer flowers and shrubs. A lovely *Prunus* × *subhirtella* 'Autumnalis' is a feature throughout the year, its first flowering in December followed by another in April, and then by the beauty of its coloured leaves in November. Living with my garden, I also need it to live for me at all seasons.

The second chamber lies beyond, on the other side of an old ivy hedge which had to be trimmed and opened for the next garden to be reached. There a maze of paths weaves around an irregularly shaped pool full of water-lilies and goldfish. I like water in a garden – life came out of water, as did Venus and all the reflections of diversity on earth. Wary doves drink from the pool in small pecks and the cat gazes longingly at the liquid surface that separates it from the fish; the tiniest debris serves as a raft for the dragonflies. Here and there a few old apple trees create a necessary vertical structure in the maze. They also provide support for rambling roses such as 'Wedding Day', for clematis, honeysuckle and hydrangeas. The ground is overgrown with perennials, among which the beautiful *Helleborus orientalis* flower in different colours in February. At all heights between and

under the boughs of the apple trees, rhododendrons, daphnes, pieris, hamamelis and a rare *Xanthoceras sorbifolium* create a profusion of vegetation throughout the seasons.

But one must always find a way out of a maze. An arched opening in the yew hedge where two topiary peacocks perch opens out into quite another world: the restful view of a meadow full of wild flowers in the spring, a peaceful open expanse of grass from which to watch the clouds chase across the sky on the west wind.

This meadow is surrounded by trees selected for their autumn colours: prunus, euonymus, acers, nyssas, sweet gums, the blazing foliage of which is reflected in a small pond dug in the grass. Like wet hair, long trailing grasses float around its outer edges.

Beyond the water another secret place, a bower overgrown with roses, shelters a stone bench. In summer, two large pots of flowering agapanthus stand on either side, their blue colour matching the flower garlands of a panel of azuleijos tiles placed at the back of the bower. Two centuries and two thousand kilometres separate this panel from its home in Portugal, where it originated before it was brought northwards to the Perche in France.

Enveloped in silence, it is a place for contemplation and meditation, although one may sometimes catch, like the

The Italian garden in July, secluded behind clipped prunus hedges, with a vista towards the magnificent *Cornus controversa* 'Variegata', a breathtaking sight when its layered branches are in full leaf. This sunny yellow theme is echoed in the carpet of low-growing plants surrounding the truncated stone column, interspersed with occasional flashes of bright colour from white, pink and purple flowers.

sound of distant thunder, the harsh calls of the wild geese drawing a faultless triangle in the sky as they head for the south. I have never heard them pass over the garden without feeling a surge of primeval excitement urging me to respond to their southward call. Yet I do not move much further than the Italian Garden enclosed in its *Prunus cerasifera* 'Pissardii' hedge. Even in winter it is enlivened by the colours of golden dwarf conifers, yellow-leaved heathers, *Mahonia japonica* 'Bealei', *Lonicera nitida* 'Baggesen's Gold', and for the rest of the year by a variety of colours from cream-whites and yellows to bright oranges.

A paved path between two low walls overflowing with creeping plants leads back towards the house, to a small orangery and two rectangular pools glimpsed through a gate and the vault of an old pleached hornbeam *allée*. Yet another walled garden filled with azaleas, rhododendrons, cornus and berberis beckons – unless you choose to turn right under the hornbeams, passing through a kind of grotto over which ferns and ivy branches hang over bizarrely shaped stones, flint extracted from some long-vanished quarry. From the darkness, one emerges into the latest of my gardens, started in 1988, which promises to grow almost into a small wood.

A wide grass lane lined on either side by standard prunus and malus trees continues the hornbeam *allée* and leads to a

Misty purples and pinks cover the old garden walls. *Kolkwitzia amabilis* 'Pink Cloud' cascades over, and *Clematis* 'Doctor Ruppel' is a mass of flowers in front of its ivy screen. The water-lily pool is edged by rock roses and catmint. Sheltered in a green bower dotted with roses, an antique dolphin from Italy has survived the winter frosts of northern France.

round pool backed by a clipped yew hedge. Two vases, one ancient and the other by Peter Wolkonsky, stand at either end of the prospect of Solvène's Garden, named after my granddaughter. On each side of this central lane, a wide variety of young trees have been planted, some for April, others for the end of summer and for autumn.

Spring gardens, summer gardens, autumn gardens, they all offer the secret of their beauty, the lost secret of Paradise.

From early morning, when the plants awaken and shake off the dew like a bird ruffling its feathers, to the coming of night, when scents swim on the nocturnal air and white flowers resemble ghostly white veils floating in an almost invisible world, who can follow in this mysterious realm the dreams and thoughts of a gardener? Yet, from this span of time, so very brief both for the garden and for himself, the gardener perceives a sign of eternity.

COMTESSE D'ANDLAU, REMALARD, FRANCE

XXXII

THE GARDEN BY THE SEA

A stone lamp-lit path disappears under cascading rhododendrons.

T HE WIDE, ever-changing view of the sea with the sounds of wind, waves and birds impressed me from the moment I saw this house and garden. Then I noticed the steep slopes, the great rock outcrops and the shelter belts of large old native conifers hiding the houses on either side. The long and narrow plot – 200 by 75 feet – gave me an opportunity to make a series of enclosed and secluded small gardens.

Over the fifteen years I have worked here with such pleasure, I have tried to create elements of surprise: go around a corner, or up a path behind a rhododendron, or a stand of bamboo, and a little secret area appears, peaceful and quiet. This is what I have striven for and hope I have achieved. I like to grow strange and amusing plants such as *Euphorbia myrsinites*, the mouse tail plant (*Arisarum proboscideum*) and varieties of sempervivum to give a light touch.

A curving stone pathway separates the nearly vertical upper and lower rock faces. Over these hangs a fine old *Wisteria floribunda*. The color of the long racemes is set off by the gray stone and the afternoon sun makes reflections of the pinnate leaves as they move in the sea breeze. Later in the season, a single vivid pink rose threads itself over the wisteria's stout branches. A large pink *Camellia sasanqua* begins to flower in early November and enjoys leaning against the warm rock; *Iris ensata* (syn. *I. kaempferi*) grows in the

seepage nearby. Very little of all this abundance can be seen from the street below.

Just here, a stranger might easily miss the way into the first small garden where a flat stone mossy area sets off a natural pool and a waterfall fed by seepage from the mountains far above. Maidenhair ferns thrive with other varieties, while the heavy rounded leaves and white flowers of *Bergenia* 'Silberlicht' give interesting contrast. Shafts of sunlight glancing through the *Cryptomeria japonica* and *Rhus typhina* 'Laciniata' make shifting reflections on the pool. Add to this the sound of the waterfall and the corner becomes a magical peaceful place. Friends coming in here and sit quietly on the stone wall by the pool while I keep my eyes open for any signs of a shrub that needs pruning or moving.

As you climb higher, an open, sunny garden appears in front of the house. Here I have made a small perennial border and a free-form rock garden of alpine plants and other treasures, mostly grown from seed offered by seed exchanges. Some stay for years while others vanish in a year or less, leaving only a label to remind me of what might have been. A tall *Cedrus deodara*, kept pruned in an open shape, allows a view of the sea and prevents the feeling that one might fall over the steep drop. This is yet another garden, equally private, enhanced by a borrowed view of native conifers.

A set of simple stone and split log steps is here transformed into a hanging garden – terraces for low and modest clumps of primulas, pulmonaria, crocosmia and foxgloves. This pathway to the wild garden is crowned by an inviting, crimson-red *Rhododendron* 'Elizabeth' at its head, a dramatic concentration of colour that is heralded by the pale but showy blooms of *R.* 'Loderi King George'.

Behind the house, a small curving lawn is surrounded by glossy-leaved rhododendrons and camellias. I chose the hostas and perennials that I planted among them as much for their differing leaves as for their muted colours. *Liquidambar styraciflua* and *Cercidiphylum japonicum* add height and good fall color; their singular leaves cast dramatic shadows on the grass, inviting an upward look to see what creates this pattern.

Leading upwards once again, perilous stone and split-log steps provide an entrance to a wild garden where hellebores

ABOVE: In a range of rich yet compatible colours, the garden opens out into a sunny lawn ringed with rhododendrons and camellias in a range of rich colours. In the foreground a fringe of foliage – stachys, colchicum and astilbe – is enlivened by the occasional outrider, such as a purple *Hyacinthoides hispanica*. RIGHT: Mountain-fed streams trickle through ferns and mossy rocks into the natural pool.

bloom early in the year and patches of *Anemone nemorosa* and *Primula veris* grow in and around the sweet-scented *Sarcococca confusa*. An old maple stump is well disguised by *Hydrangea anomala* subsp. *petiolaris* and species clematis. Peace and quiet are maintained by evergreen shrubs which deaden the traffic noise of the nearby road.

I value my garden as a private and tranquil place of many diverse spaces and for the surprises each contains. The chief joy of the garden is its continuing state of becoming, the fact that it is never complete.

ELAINE CORBET, WEST VANCOUVER, CANADA

XXXIII

A Tale of Three Sisters

Inside the gate, roses, ferns and orchids greet the summer visitor.

To visit this lovely small garden, perched on a steep hillside overlooking Porth Neigwl – perhaps better known as Hell's Mouth Bay – on the Llŷn peninsula, is to have all of one's senses aroused. The colours, scents and sounds in the garden are quite stunning, and once through the gate the visitor feels removed from the bustle of the outside world. The atmosphere of tranquillity that captures and enfolds the visitor is perhaps what gives Plas-yn-Rhiw its secret quality.

Set in a dramatic landscape with distant views of Cader Idris to the south, mighty Snowdon in the east, and Bardsey Island to the west, the house and garden are protected from the prevailing north-west wind by Rhiw mountain, and by the ancient wood that surrounds the property. Now owned by the National Trust, it was once a busy working farm.

It is easy to suppose that each successive mistress of Plas-yn-Rhiw would grow a few flowers, in addition to fruit and vegetables, just to make the immediate surroundings look pretty, but there are no formal plans of layout or planting ideas. It is a garden that has slowly evolved over many years, planted with whatever was available.

The first hint of a formal layout was discernible only at the beginning of this century, when the lady of the house at that time, living abroad each winter, was possibly influenced by what she had seen in Italy. She may well have planted the little parterre

LEFT: Half-concealed among foliage and dwarfed by a huge laurel tree, the old stable-cum-tackroom has a fox weather vane. OVERLEAF: The old woodland, which so much appealed to the three sisters who bought the estate in the 1930s, blends imperceptibly into the cultivated parts. The stately eucryphia in the middle background is a mass of blossom among the surrounding trees in August.

garden, but for many years after her departure the garden lay neglected and the garden returned to its wild state.

In the late 1930s, the Keating sisters bought the estate. Slowly, and with much thought and care, they restored and enlarged the garden. The three women were enchanted by the unspoiled beauty of the whole area, and treasured the old woodland surrounding the house and garden, with its rich bird life filling the air with song, and the ever-changing carpets of flowers covering the woodland floor from early spring to high summer.

The sisters had vision and determination, and managed to create a garden which brings comfort and a sense of peace, where nothing is harsh or restrictively formal. The temperate climate provides the right conditions for some rare and unusual plants, and it is not surprising to see a few roses and fuchsias in bloom in December. *Fuchsia magellanica*, attaining tree-like proportions, is a sight to behold when in full flower.

The normal route into the garden takes the visitor past the house, and here by the side of the verandah is a fine specimen of *Abutilon* 'Ashford Red' growing happily in the open. The summer jasmine either side of the front door accommodates nests of blue tits and wrens, and the lovely scent of the old 'Zéphirine Drouhin' rose growing up the pillar of the verandah creates a sense of timelessness.

In spring this garden is ablaze with colour. There are camellias in abundance, and the magnolias are a splendid sight, especially *Magnolia campbellii* subsp. *mollicomata* with its lovely grey-green bark and huge pink flowers, followed by most unusual seed pods. Rhododendrons and azaleas dazzle in the bright sunlight, and everywhere underfoot are wild primroses, violets and celandines. The old Irish yews provide deep colour and contrast to the flower beds, enclosed by their little box hedges. Lilies, roses, iris, forget-me-nots, joined later in the season by verbenas, potentillas and many more, grow in a harmonious jumble.

In summer a callistemon with its bright red bottlebrush flowers is neighbour to a huge honey-scented euphorbia, while a little further on a pieris seems to be growing out of the old apple tree. Meander along a short yew-lined path to emerge once more into bright sunlight; here the paths are wider, and one can sit for a while on a sun-warmed stone seat and look out to sea. It is difficult to believe that this bit of paradise was once raided by Norsemen.

In this part of the garden the philadelphus, when in flower, fills the air with its beautiful scent. At other times it is the flower-laden corylopsis that pleases the eye or the

LEFT: Tucked into a steep hillside, a wrought-iron seat takes its shelter from a clipped hedge. Cistus and bergenia impale themselves on its metalwork. ABOVE: Traditional cottage flowers – roses, tradescantia, kniphofia – make an early summer show below the old farmhouse. The flourishing *Magnolia campbellii* ssp. *mollicomata* in the background was planted by the Keating sisters in 1947.

pittosporum that holds one spellbound with its remarkable profusion of almost black flowers. In late August the stately eucryphia, smothered in large white flowers, shines like a beacon, and the warm lanterns of the crinodendron glow amid the dark foliage. There are hundreds more plants and shrubs, the natural and the cultivated blending and providing a rich habitat for wildlife.

Near the house is a beautiful little cobbled courtyard where an old wisteria in bloom hangs like a purple curtain, hiding what was once a dairy. Rose, honeysuckle, clematis and aubrieta add their scent and hue. The little stream, which in the distant past powered an old mill, provides sweet music in summer before disappearing under the garden and out to sea; its winter song can be a mighty roar. In the short winter days, the birds make the most of the daylight hours by feasting off the rich harvest of berries and fruit. A pale pink viburnum glows in the fading light, and *Garrya elliptica*, now at its best, provides cover for the little wren. At dusk, one may be lucky enough to see the old dog fox as he lopes through the garden on his way home. The garden, now hushed and quiet, lies hidden among the trees to await the spring, when it will delight the visitor once more.

MADELEINE DICK, PLAS-YN-RHIW, GWYNEDD

XXXIV

ARTIST'S IMPRESSIONS

In midsummer, bold-leaved hostas take over from meconopsis.

'Promise me you will never say
You should have seen my garden yesterday'

SIR CHARLES FRASER:

Y OU SHOULD, however, have seen ours when we were househunting in 1957. We looked at a variety of flats and then saw an advertisement for Shepherd House. One look at the tumbledown 1690s house was enough for me. We made a quick inspection of what had once been a garden and spoke to a youngster prowling in the knee-high weeds. When asked what he was doing, 'shooting rats', was the none too encouraging reply. 'That was a waste of time,' I said as we drove away. Ann took a different view.

Inveresk is an unusual seventeenth- and eighteenth-century village built on the site of a large Roman camp. The name Inver is Celtic for 'at the mouth of', and Esk derives from the Celtic word for water. There are many rivers with that derivation, and of course whisky has the same origin. Little is known of Inveresk from Roman times until the seventeenth century, but a number of merchants' houses were built there, amongst them Shepherd House; its Dutch gable, evidence of the links between the Forth Ports and the Low Countries in the sixteenth and seventeenth centuries.

In the two potagers – once a conventional vegetable garden – pink 'Dreaming Maid' tulips pierce through a carpet of forget-me-nots under the skeletal framework of the pergola, which later in the season will support runner beans and sweet peas. The central path is lined with catmint, and *Prunus* 'Kanzan' and ancient apple trees flower above drifts of flowers and foliage, with the orchard in the background.

Gardening is probably a genetic disease and I certainly inherited it. So I set about digging a vegetable patch. A lawn was mown and served as a rugby and cricket pitch for our four sons. I gave half the vegetable garden to Robin White, an agronomist. It was galling to see his vegetables grow to twice the size of mine, but fun to tell friends that I had an agronomist advising me in my garden.

For some years the garden remained a place to play, where boys and vegetables flourished, but the four sons grew up, the lawn was no longer the site of the Calcutta Cup and Test Matches, and even croquet, the cause of so many family squabbles, was played less often. Ann's artist's eye planned more and more changes. On the whole we ended up agreeing, but there was a good deal of disagreement *en route*. I was not a little concerned when I first heard her thoughts of requisitioning my conventional vegetable garden, with its regimented lines of cabbages. Now I am rather proud of my potager.

Visits to other gardens gave us ideas, and gradually today's layout evolved. If the eye for design and the

knowledge of plants is Ann's, I wonder what my contribution has been. My mother would walk round the garden and conclude her tour with the comment 'What a work!' On the contrary, it has not been work but the greatest possible fun.

Is it a secret garden? A secret is 'knowledge kept from others', but our garden is in fact shared with many. Ann, however, may see it differently.

The winding grass path invites eyes and feet to stray past pale flowers of *Smilacina racemosa*, rounded foliage of *Ballota pseudodictamnus* and tall heads of *Euphorbia characias*, thriving in the dry area beneath a large Scots pine. Deep pink 'Attila' tulips raise their heads above the sun-dappled path, with *Rhododendron* 'Loderi King George' a pale reflection and reminder in the background.

LADY FRASER:

'WHERE YOU TEND a rose, a thistle cannot grow' is an apt quotation for our style of gardening. We plant so intensively that there is hardly a square inch of bare earth for weeds; in fact I wonder if the garden at Shepherd House were left undisturbed for a decade, it would resemble the magical and mysterious secret garden of Frances Hodgson Burnett's novel from which my quotation was taken. There are many similarities: the high stone walls, the single entrance door, the roses climbing up the old apple trees, the winding grass paths and the curtains of ivy, all of which created such a mystical atmosphere for Mary Lennox when she first entered that romantic and magical garden.

A romantic garden requires a formal framework. With this in mind and with the help of countless books, our garden has gradually evolved. The end of the child-dominated years was marked by the demolition of their playroom in 1984 and the building of a conservatory in its place. This was the starting point of what has, over the years, become a passion.

Our first attempts at design were to restore the central path shown on eighteenth-century maps and to transform an area dominated by two very boring beds of Floribunda roses into an old-fashioned herb garden, our intention being to fill it with plants that might have been grown when the house was built; even the *Euphorbia characias* which has seeded profusely in this area might have been there then. I am not sure, however, that all the plants chosen qualify – certainly the standard 'Iceberg' roses fail that test.

Every garden needs a focal point. We already had a vista from the house through the now completed old-fashioned garden, across the lawn and up the nepeta-lined grass path towards the boundary wall, but somehow the eye never made it beyond the lawn. We decided that a formal rectangular pond, the same width as the path, would lead the eye on and at the same time provide a focal point. A later addition was a bronze fountain by Gerald Ogilvie Laing of a girl washing her

hair. With its reflections and the soothing sound of constantly falling water, the pond has given an added dimension to the garden as a whole.

The beds on either side of the lawn are curved and luxuriantly planted to contrast with the formality of the pond. The left-hand bed contains mainly 'hot' colours – oriental poppies, underplanted with tiger lilies to extend the flowering period, red aquilegias, parrot tulips, apricot foxgloves, bronze and apricot violas, including 'Irish Molly'. Accents of gold come with *Anthemis tinctoria* 'E. C. Buxton', *Physocarpus opulifolius* 'Dart's Gold', *Weigela middendorffiana*, and *Arbutus unedo* and *Aralia elata* give height. By contrast, the bed on the opposite side of the lawn contains the cool blues, violets, magentas and purples of

Pots of standard fuchsias, osteospermums, agapanthus, petunias and lilies stand on the terrace outside the conservatory. Steps half-submerged in *Cotoneaster horizontalis* and *Clematis alpina* 'Frances Rivis' lead from this secluded area to the upper lawn planted with wall and island borders. It is a painter's garden, formal in framework, romantic in overlay; its colours, shapes and textures applied with a sure and skilful hand.

hardy geraniums, campanulas, salvias, agapanthus, hebes and violas. *Robinia pseudoacacia* 'Frisia', underplanted with purple cotinus, provides height and contrast.

The central grass path, which in full summer becomes almost a tunnel with four rose-, honeysuckle- and vine-clad arches, leads to further 'rooms' – a symmetrical potager, a white garden, a shrubbery planted on the site of an old byre, and a shaded garden inspired by the distinguished artist Ian Hamilton Findlay. Here cyclamen, ferns and periwinkles flourish under a canopy created by a wellingtonia and other trees planted twenty-five years ago. As the years pass and the canopy grows denser, this has become the most secret place in our secret garden.

SIR CHARLES AND LADY FRASER, INVERESK, MIDLOTHIAN

XXXV

THE MILL ON THE WINDRUSH

Jeremy, Jemima and Doris stand guard by the mill race.

Oɴ ᴀ ᴄᴏʟᴅ ᴊᴀɴᴜᴀʀʏ ᴅᴀʏ, a most unpropitious time for house-hunting, I saw Little Aston Mill. It was love at first sight. Set in a valley on the River Windrush, the mill house was listed as a site in the Domesday Book of 1086; the present Cotswold stone mill and its mill race, dating from 1303-5, were positioned so that the lower ground near the river provided shelter, the meadows along its banks contributing to the beauty of this gentle stretch of water.

As I walked thorough the woods towards the point where river and mill race divide – a long, narrow strip of land bounded by water – the sound of rushing water and of wood animals scurrying through the wild rhubarb, and the sight of the bleak bare native willows with their branches hanging forlorn, beckoned me further into this enchanted world. It was alive, untamed and very beautiful, and I resolved to make it my secret garden.

That was three years ago. I was bursting with ideas. My experience of horticulture was limited to the tropical garden of my previous home in Singapore, but I was undaunted, even though I recognized that in the making of a seven-acre garden there was a great deal of work to be done, especially considering the limy, stony soil, the frosty Cotswold winters and the thriving wildlife – foxes, badgers, squirrels, moles and deer. I enlisted the help of Helen

Hockey, a landscape gardener whose sense of colour and style in planting I admired, and together we set about creating a much enlarged garden.

First, we took stock of what my predecessors had left me. Immediately surrounding the mill were old borders in dire need of attention, but which nevertheless contained some established specimen trees and shrubs. Among them were the lovely grey *Pyrus salicifolia* 'Pendula', *Hydrangea aspera, Viburnum × bodnantense* 'Dawn', the sweetly scented old rose 'Reine Victoria', a beautiful weeping *Prunus pendula* 'Pendula Rosea', strategically placed by the water's edge, and a grouping of several of what has become my favourite tree, *Betula utilis* var. *jacquemontii*.

Linking the entranceway to the mill were hedges of copper beech, with another semi-circular copper beech hedge planted as a screen, in an apparent attempt to create a garden room close to the house front.

Competing for attention on the main façade were a vigorous rose, 'Climbing Etoile de Hollande', a century-old espaliered pear tree still bearing delicious fruit, a lovely yellow winter-flowering jasmine, a *Clematis montana* 'Tetrarose', and the big surprise, a well-established *Passiflora caerulea*. So we had a good structure to work from, but the existing garden encompassed less than an acre.

At the heart of the garden a seat is positioned to take full advantage of the view towards the main bed – a riot of colourful mixed cranesbill geraniums, roses and alchemilla. Maples provide more dominant colour. In the foreground, shade comes from the fan-like light and dark-green leaves of *Acer platanoides* 'Drummondii', with the shrimp-pink leaves of *A. pseudoplatanus* 'Brilliantissimum in the background.

We started in the spring of 1990, upgrading and filling in the old borders, weeding the beds thoroughly and rearranging any existing plants. We added some roses and herbaceous plants, and tulips for the following spring – 'China Pink', 'Bellona' and, darkest of all, 'Queen of the Night'. The garden room at the mill front was greatly improved by increasing the height of the existing Cotswold stone wall in proportion to the semi-circular copper beech hedge. Behind this heightened wall we created a larger secret garden, approached by a tunnel of wrought-iron archways covered alternately with climbing roses – 'Lavinia', 'Swan Lake', 'Rambling Rector' and 'Handel' – and with 'James Grieve' apples and 'Comice' and 'Conference' pears. At the foot of each of the archways we planted mixed hostas, *Alchemilla mollis*, santolina and assorted small campanulas, underplanted with 'Spring Green' and pink 'Angélique' tulips.

At the end of the archways stretched a vista of rolling meadowland bounded at the bottom by 200 metres of the Windrush, but in its natural state the river did not yield the full benefit of its spectacular view. To achieve this, we remoulded the landscape, creating three different levels of flattened land. On the upper level we designed a knot garden, a pattern of four rectangular shapes crossing at the centre. We used five-year-old box hedging, and filled the compartments

The mellowness of an English midsummer – the mill and its race bathed in sunlight filtered through the branches of a weeping ash which stretch right down into the water. In the shadow of the simple, rustic wooden bridge flourish the wild plants and flowers of water-fed meadows: grasses, coltsfoot, ferns, kingcups and cornus line the mill race in the lowest part of the wild garden.

with 'Little White Pet' and 'The Fairy' roses, 'Munstead' lavender and santolina, underplanted for spring with our favourite combination of 'Spring Green' and 'Angélique' tulips to echo those beneath the archways. Hedges of laurel and fast-growing Leyland cypresses secured the secrecy of this upper enclosure.

On the middle level we seeded nearly an acre of new lawn, with a softly curving edge echoing the contour of the river bank. The grass sloped gently down to the lower level, merging finally with the river, and this last level was kept mainly in its wild state, with the addition only of willows, narcissi and water-loving plants, for the flow of the formal into the natural was essential to achieve the look of timelessness.

At the north-western side of the mill, an acre of raw pastureland inclined down to the mill race. The enclosure became our secret spring garden, the main seasonal focus provided by an avenue of ornamental spring and autumn trees and shrub roses leading to a five-pillared stone temple. We planted an assortment of twelve thousand bulbs, none exceeding a foot in height, in tightly knit groups – *Narcissus* 'Tête-à-tête' and *N. bulbocodium*, white and blue muscari, *Fritillaria meleagris*, and blue and white *Anemone blanda*. The following year the overall effect was breathtakingly spectacular, a marvellous instant display.

Further up in the mill race, towards the woods, is our best-kept secret. Bounded by water and further surrounded by trees, it is nature's hidden world, invisible to man's prying eyes – a long and narrow strip of about three acres, blessed with rich moist soil in which plants like native irises, wild rhubarb, water marigolds, ferns, wild orchids, grasses and assorted other wildflowers thrive. It already contained an assortment of trees such as ash, lime, horse chestnut and native willows, but some of these were in a terminal state of neglect.

We realized the importance of keeping to William Robinson's concept of natural planting – striking the right balance of an idealized wilderness in which man, not nature, is in control – so we cleared the area of fallen branches, dead trees and overgrown grasses, and designated sections for mown paths, mindful of not cutting until the wild flowers had bloomed and re-seeded. Here we planted primulas, foxgloves, water-loving plants and bulbs with a special affinity for

As the mill race surges from beneath the mill, the planting becomes more garden-like. The border includes lime-green alchemilla, mauve meadow rue, white campanula, pink scabious and yellow kerria. All the trees, including amelanchier and cercidiphyllum, have been planted for the glory of their autumn colour. The mill itself has *Hydrangea petiolaris* growing by its garden entrance.

woodland; I treasured the carpets of snowdrops and winter aconites which emerged in the early spring. Shrubs such as *Viburnum plicatum*, variegated dogwood, *Mahonia × media*, and shrub roses – 'Complicata', 'Constance Spry' *R. glauca* (syn. *R. rubrifolia*) blend in happily. Wood animals still roam, but respect our sanctuary.

At present we are planting a new young breed of trees to replace the old and dying, concentrating on the small and the ornamental: *Cornus controversa*, West Himalayan birch, Japanese acer, and several species of malus and prunus, the more majestic sorbus species, evergreens, dwarf and large blue picea, *Cedrus atlantica* 'Glauca'; and trees for posterity: ginkgo, red oak and the lovely tulip tree. My young trees are my children, to be nurtured, protected and prepared for the adult lives ahead of them.

Until then our secret gardens, although giving wonderful displays, will not be fully mature and fortunately many more years of exciting challenge await us.

LULETTE MONBIOT, BOURTON ON THE WATER, GLOUCESTERSHIRE

XXXVI

INFINITE PROJECTS

A woodland fringe meeting of rhododendron and meconopsis.

I AM A GREEDY gardener. By 1982 a city lot was no longer large enough for me, and fortunately my partner Ralph Hastings was inspired by a similar dream of country living and infinite projects.

When we found it, our ten-acre property on Whidbey Island had 'capabilities'. Its potential took some imagination, however, as it was partially second-growth forest, partially pasture scattered with old debris. Sloping to the west, the land dropped into wetlands filled with wildlife.

In our Pacific north-west, country living can be pretty close to pioneering. We designed and built our own house; before we could even start to create the garden we had to clear trees and erect fences, but we were free to use all the varied habitats our land offered, making of it what we would enjoy, while respecting what was already there. I wanted everything.

I wanted domestic pets, farm animals, wild animals, birds. I wanted pastures and orchards and a wood lot, native forest, undisturbed wetland, ornamental gardens. I wanted to make a peaty bog bed, a flowering meadow, a shady border, an alpine rockery, herbaceous borders, and to eat my way through vegetable beds, fruit trees and a strawberry patch. I wanted to use plants and ideas from Asian, English, Moorish, Italian and American Midwest gardeners. I wanted seclusion, quiet and nature; friends and an absolute riot of color.

I didn't compromise much. With an overall small scale, and each border or theme an incident within it, we are able to enjoy a wide variety. Our house is 1100 square feet, the sheep flock numbers four, and the herbaceous perennial Helen Van Pelt Wilson Memorial Border is forty feet long. There is a continuous series of beds and areas, sometimes defined by low hedges, changes of level or trees, but never walled off into separate rooms. Like a small house with an open floor plan, these spaces allow longer views and make the whole garden appear much larger.

The garden itself has a spacious feeling, but it is hidden from the outside world. Driving by on a little country road, you see only a hedgerow-edged pasture dotted with sheep. But venture along the curved drive, through the gate, pass around three magnificent *Thuja plicata*, and another world appears below.

We left the outside edges untouched, as well as four acres of mixed forest of western hemlock, Douglas fir and grand fir. Inside this green case my garden lies like jewels scattered in sparkling colors. Pastels and blues are intensified in our gray, overcast northern sky, so I use these colors widely, along with silvers and greys and other textured foliage, to form an impressionist haze, gauzy and shimmering. Accents of burgundy or violet also spread through many

Within a ten-acre garden carved out of pasture- and woodland, with wild wetland at its boundary, the house sits with the forest guarding its back. A forty-foot-long border snakes around the house, wrapping it in a pale ribbon of silver leaves and yellow and purple flowers. Double white *Rosa banksiae* has escaped to climb the tower, wafting its violet scent into the upper rooms.

Entering by the oriental-looking wooden gate, this part of the garden is planted for winter effect with dwarf conifers, heathers and the tri-coloured *Leucothoë* 'Scarletta'. The ample green leaves of *Bergenia cordifolia* 'Purpurea' emphasize the curve of the lawn. The brightest colour now comes from the terracotta pots, planted with a pair of standard *Umbellularia californica*.

parts of the garden, and this repetition of color interweaves and connects differing borders and areas. The most intensely planted garden is near the house, where it is extended by mown paths through small meadows of wild flowers and grasses, then extended even more to the eye by open pastures leading down to a large pond, and the forest beyond.

The sheep mow and fertilize the pastures and the orchard, and I take advantage of their dislike for certain plants, such as narcissus (poisonous) or digitalis and verbascum (fuzzy-leaved), by planting these in scattered clusters. The sheep are separated from the garden by an intricately cut picket fence, another fence hidden in foliage, and a ha-ha.

All year the pond is full of visiting creatures, including deer, coyote, otter, wood ducks and blue heron, and in summer it provides a cool swimming hole. The bunnies and I have an agreement: they hop through the garden, but only munch on lawn. My cat culls the old or the very young, and my Scottie dog exercises them.

A traditional clipped Irish yew hedge screens parked cars from the house and garden and acts as a backdrop to an entry area which in winter is full of color and interest. Starting in October, the fragrant *Osmanthus heterophyllus* blooms and *Tricyrtis hirta* throws its tiny lavender-spotted flowers in sprays over the walkway. Ending in February, a bank of winter heath wakes up the bees, and crocus, iris and other small bulbs spread a gold and blue carpet elsewhere. In their winter coats, the heathers *Calluna vulgaris* 'Blazeaway' and 'Aurea' are vibrant scarlet, orange and gold, surrounding *Cryptomeria japonica* 'Elegans', which turns in winter to the color of the curving brick path, while the mood of *Rhododendron* PJM is a bronzy burgundy gleam. Under the pink spread of *Prunus × subhirtella* 'Rosea', the early blooms of deciduous and white-flowered varieties of *Rhododendron mucronulatum* balance delicately on tiny stems. In summer all this becomes a green glade, cooled even more by the white variegation of a dogwood, a white-striped grass and a running strawberry with tiny white fruit.

We incorporated established native trees to help compensate for our garden's youth. *Acer macrophyllum* shades the house and is a haven for birds at our bedroom window, and a solitary Douglas fir stands sentinel at my garden shed.

As a student, I often studied out in my garden until one college year I moved my desk right out into the back yard, within reach of the raspberries, and found I could concentrate even during summer if I felt I wasn't missing out on the season. So we built our house with my office at the top of the second-floor tower with windows open to the garden on three sides. Double white *Rosa banksiae* var. *banksiae* climbs the tower and wafts its violet scent by my computer. From this perspective the knot garden and other patterns between the borders express themselves boldly.

Near the house two garden islands of mixed borders spill over with silken plants, flowering pastel and fragrant from April through October, with some winter interest. *Pyrus salicifolia* 'Pendula' centers each island, with shrubs and perennials tiering down to an edging of rue and lavender. Here, in June, *Buddleja alternifolia* 'Argentea' and *Rosa* 'Cardinal de Richelieu' mix and bloom, with *Crambe maritima* and *Stachys byzantina* 'Silver Carpet' at their feet, and tiny spheres of turquoise *Allium caeruleum* poking through. In the opposite corner, *Macleaya cordata*'s large leaves with pinkish stems, *Thalictrum glaucum*'s dainty blue-green foliage, and *Phlomis fruticosa*'s gold-sheened fuzzy leaves all form a cool backdrop to the pink eyes of *Lychnis coronaria* 'Oculata', the lavender puffs of *Limonium latifolium* and the apricot petals of *Papaver spicatum*. The round *Rhododendron yakushimanum* 'Ken Janeck' anchors the corner and add its felted gray leaves; I like to use rhododendrons in mixed borders for their foliage, shape, and fragrant foliage or flowers.

Deeper into the garden lurk other color surprises. In the partially shaded woodland corner, *Rhododendron bureaui* and its soft furry hybrid, 'Teddy Bear', are flashing cinnamon under their leaves and woolly stems, while at their feet Welsh poppies show how delicate orange can be. A grafted standard *Acer palmatum* 'Beni-schichihenge' floats its coral-orange leaves by *Rhododendrons* 'Lady Rosebery' and *R. cinnabarinum* 'Conroy', whose round blue leaves emit a spicy scent along with azaleas and day-lilies. At the back, a sculpture of peregrine falcons overlooks the small bay.

Hidden behind the house is a burgundy and gold border. Backed in part by four varieties of *Cotinus coggygria*, it glows in the western evening light, and in the afternoon sun is so bright you must squint. Behind this border the crown of *Acer platanoides* 'Crimson King' makes a black hole, and further

towards the pond a large, multiple-trunked hemlock, *Tsuga heterophylla*, spreads its dark green skirts. Masses of fragrant *Rosa* 'Graham Thomas' show for summer glamor, *Lindera obtusiloba* for autumn color, and *Taxus cuspidata* 'Bright Gold' for winter interest.

My job as a publisher's representative means that I travel throughout the Pacific north-west. Always, as I drive home, my spirits lift as I pass the towering red cedars that signal the entrance to our secret garden. Each time there are changes to note, surprises at every turn of the path.

HOLLY TURNER, WHIDBEY ISLAND, WASHINGTON STATE

XXXVII

PAST AND PRESENT INTERMINGLED

The sundial at the garden's main axis, wreathed in flowers.

By a riverside, written small, is the word 'Pitmuies'. It features on a map of 1677 showing the County of Angus, which illustrates the chronic shortage of roads. Just two existed then, 'The King's Highway betwixt Dundee and Brechin' and a coastal route, to be travelled by Dr Johnson a hundred years later. Also revealed is the scarcity of woodland but the quantity of 'mosses', bogs that would be drained in future centuries to give the rich, fertile farmland in an area that even today still appears remote and is largely unknown to the world outside.

A house is recorded at Pitmuies from a century earlier and remnants from older houses remain incorporated in the south wing of the elegant white-harled three-storey mansion. 'Mr Ogilvy's fine new house of 1730', with two late eighteenth-century bow-fronted single-storey wings, gazes serenely westward across its lawns and ha-ha to the great boled Spanish chestnuts and the dark-coloured copper beeches that flank the view and lead the eye to a further landscape of pasture and woodland. It is a stretch of unbroken green, unfussed by planting, tranquil and traditional.

A high hedge of yew runs from the corner of the house towards the river below, a barrier to the prevailing south-west wind and concealing the contrasting world of the garden behind, an entrance to which lurks through a deep-cut arch. It is reached

LEFT: A bird's eye view of the rose garden, with a fragrant hedge of *R.* 'Columbine' separating it from the central fountain pool. On the left is a phalanx of delphiniums, on the right a yellow and purple border. OVERLEAF: The trellis walk, decked with clematis and *R.* 'Fellenberg', gives passing glimpses of the Gothic wash house and washing green, now an alpine meadow carpeted with bulbs in spring.

through a small white iron gate, then a snib must be lifted to open the heavy green wooden door beyond and so reveal the burst of colour and wealth of plants that lie ahead.

Little is known of the history of the garden, but its walls still tally with those shown on an estate map of 1780 and it has long been renowned for its delphiniums. Two adjoining walled gardens, flat and square, are overlooked respectively by the back and side windows of the house. The smaller garden, lying behind, contains gnarled old fruit trees and still produces table fruit and vegetables, as well as cut flowers, for the house, while the fruit trees also play host to spring-flowering clematis, intermingling with their blossom. The 'cottage borders' below are box-edged and planted first for a spring display and then goaded into summer with emerging sweet Williams and penstemons, interspersed with annuals. The mellow old walls behind are loaded with climbing roses and honeysuckles.

A gateway leads through the dividing wall into the greater second garden, its pair of white iron gates always open to beckon you on to the archway of silver weeping pear which frames the main herbaceous borders. Planted in soft colours, predominately old-fashioned shades of pink, with white and a lot of grey foliage, these borders are backed by a vigorous red hedge of *Prunus cerasifera*

153

A dramatic archway of silver-leaved *Pyrus salicifolia*
'Pendula' in its woolly July exuberance frames an *allée*
of flowers, their colours graduating from white and
pink to strong yellow and purple. The beds are inter-
rupted by the sundial at the cross-axis before they funnel out towards countryside and woodland. Self-sown
fennel lends the sundial a misty, distant look.

'Pissardii'. This is cut down each autumn to its squat, square winter shape, and springs into growth with the emerging herbaceous plants the following year. By midsummer it backs a funnel of flowers enclosing and enveloping the visitor who walks down to the central sundial and on towards the tall narrow final gateway. In July, over the backdrop of red branches, peer the tall spikes of the delphiniums – thousands of heads, ten to eleven feet high, that run from the borders of plants five deep the whole length of the garden. These are descendants of the delphiniums introduced after the First World War; most are 'nameless', awaiting identification.

The formal rose garden, with its beds of Hybrid Teas and Floribundas, lies to the right of the massed delphiniums. Favourite amongst them must be *R.* 'Colombine', delicate and sweet-smelling, the colour of 'Peace', now appears to be obsolete from growers' catalogues but remains cherished here; entwined by white *Viola cornuta*, it fills two hedge beds above the central pool and fountain. Shrub roses and a fence of rambling roses tumble alongside the formal area, culminating in a circular bed of *R.* 'Iceberg' underplanted with coal-black pansies and overlooked by a white rose arbour.

At the foot of the rose garden, a trellis walk leads both ways. To the right, it swings round past an old carved stone bench and into the vista of the blue and soft yellow double borders which lead back, the length of the garden, to the house and its drawingroom window. Through this window, house and garden unite, with pale blue walls, sofas of thalictrum yellow and lampshades of delphinium blue harmonizing with and being echoed in the view outside.

Turn left along the trellis walk with its festoons of clematis and climbing roses, and you come to the great exuberant masses of sweet-smelling *R.* 'Goldfinch' which flank the pillar gates and the two large bushes of *R.* × *centifolia* opposite. Here, earlier in summer, peonies and aquilegias have predominated and in the bed along the trellis walk, meconopsis, martagon lilies, hostas, exotic ferns and bergenias flourish. Alongside this walk a row of eight *Prunus serrula* planted in 1985 are now a fine feature with their lovely red polished bark that just calls to be stroked as you pass by.

Three steps above them, the former tennis court sports four paved corners – a suitable habitat for the collection of laced and feathered dianthus and the many violas, including the charming ladies 'Maggie Mott' and 'Irish Molly'. This is edged with a border of mixed catmint and alchemilla, enhanced by the old dark red rose 'Charles de Mills' spreading himself through them. The court centre has a raised bed of pink, buff and cream potentillas, with the green spikes of galtonias ready to break into a fountain towards summer's end.

There are so many shrubs and alpines, but two huge *Photinia davidiana* dominate. Hoherias, euphorbias and eryngiums, grow among unusual and rare plants, or forms, and many others grown for foliage alone. Every space is crammed, so that plants jostle and fall over each other in a natural way.

Outside the original garden and below the trellis fence lies a double rose walk – *rugosas* underplanted with peonies and sweet Williams on one side and old moss and striped roses with a mixture of penstemons on the other. This rose-edged grass terrace forms one side of the 'alpine meadow', carpeted in spring by early mauve and white crocus and then by larger bulbs, inheritors of the washing and drying green spread before a quaint little Gothick building, first mentioned in an estate plan of 1814 as 'Wash House' but often mistaken for a chapel on account of its shape and mullioned windows.

Part of the charm of Pitmuies must lie in its little ancillary buildings, all in the vicinity of the house and all roofed with stone slates. Perhaps pride of place must go to the turreted doo'cot on the riverside, a pigeon house replete with towers, a thousand nesting boxes and boasting a weathered marriage stone, with Ogilvy and Guthrie quarterings and the date 1643, with runner-up the long low 'blackhouse', its fern-encrusted roof dripping moisture on to *Primula florindae* below. It culminates in the dog kennel and a date stone of 1775. These eighteenth-century farm buildings form the backdrop to more gardening and give the atmosphere of seclusion and secrecy that seems to pervade the garden, where the past intermingles with the present.

MARGARET OGILVIE, HOUSE OF PITMUIES, ANGUS

XXXVIII

SANCTUARY FROM THE CITY

Purple-veined and golden-eyed *Iris ensata* 'Nikko'.

Private, hidden, concealed, kept from view – my garden is secret both physically and metaphysically. It occupies an intimate part of my life, separate and quite distinct from my pressured existence as a partner in a major New York law firm. My secret passion, it keeps me sane – unless we agree that all passionate gardeners are really a little crazy.

The garden itself is tucked behind our eighteenth-century clapboard farmhouse, between the house and a weathered barn and within the confines of old walls and split-rail fencing. When we first bought the house over twenty years ago, there was no garden, but there were wonderful old irregular dry-stone walls. Our first task was to clear away the scrub and lilacs that had grown into a small forest separating the house from the barn. Interestingly, the only garden plants that had survived the decades of neglect were an old rambling rose (unidentified to this day), clumps of *Paeonia lactiflora* 'Festiva Maxima', which are still going strong, and groups of *Iris pallida*, wild flag iris, tradescantia and *Hemerocallis fulva*. The acid soil was basically gravel and we soon discovered that we were in a cold pocket where temperatures can go as low as −25° Fahrenheit.

My artist husband became my Capability Brown, transforming an old gravel pit into a new pond, moving hills and roads, removing woods, levelling lawns and constructing stone walls. He claimed he was pro-

Inspired by the golden garden at Crathes Castle in Scotland, yellow, purple and grey plants surround the fountain-basin. Water flows from the mouth of a frog held by a young girl and cascades into the stone pool, its spray mingling with the sprays of *Heuchera micrantha* 'Palace Purple'. *Verbascum olympicum* and *Yucca flaccida* 'Golden Sword' add height and drama to the mounds of soft foliage.

viding me with new canvases to paint with plants. It was he who bulldozed out the lilac forest I had tried to restore, leaving me with a muddy mess, so that I was forced to become more expansive and ambitious in my efforts.

The intimate, intensely gardened part now includes herbaceous borders set against the rambling walls, a rose walk leading to a garden shed, and a fountain garden, with a new terraced garden under construction. As I am coping with this only on weekends with the help of one person one day a week, I am certainly over-extended.

The first herbaceous border was planted around the existing peony, which responded beautifully to its liberation from weeds. This border is best in the early spring, with its intense blue *Iris sibirica* and herbaceous peonies in shades of white, pink and deep rose, following the blowsy blooms of the tree peonies. The larger herbaceous border is set between two stone walls backed by the gray barn, and peaks later in the summer in tones of white, purple, blue and pink with touches of gray, and a little yellow here and there that I simply didn't have the heart to rip out.

Inspired by the old rose that had survived, I added the rose walk over ten years ago, choosing old, tough roses primarily for their hardiness and fragrance. There are over fifty rose bushes, flanked by climbers growing on cedar posts within two

stone walls and edged with *Nepeta* 'Six Hills Giant'. Because most of the roses bloom only once, in June, I encourage *Nicotiana alata* to self-seed between the roses, so that their white wands continue to provide fragrance into the summer along with a few repeat bloomers. *Rosa.* 'Thérèse Bugnet' is the first and most consistent of these, with 'Rose de Rescht', 'Comte de Chambord', *R. gallica* var. *officinalis* and many others, including my newest experiments with the David Austin roses. Among the climbers *R.* 'New Dawn' and its parent, 'Doctor W. Van Fleet', perform superbly, but I love most the subtle apricot-to-gold colors of 'Goldbusch'. Sadly, most of the climbers that tolerate our cold climate are not particularly fragrant.

When we added to our house two years ago, the garden had to expand accordingly. Our 'moon garden' features my latest folly, a fountain, and the sound of water now seems indispensable to the balance and serenity of the garden.

In the mist of an early June morning, twin drifts of purple nepeta lead the eye along a grass path to a wide-doored, trellissed summerhouse. Old roses float above the catmint border and, above them climbing roses chosen for their hardiness and fragrance grow over a cedar post-and-rail fence between two stone walls. Just visible in the distance is the stone figure of the water maiden.

When I consulted a neighbor about fountain construction, he not only responded but gave me a statue of a young girl holding a frog, which is now set in a small pool, with rough stones to keep from too much formality in our country setting. I have tried to use yellow foliage and textures here, accented with purples and grays, because of the wonderful golden garden we loved so much at Crathes Castle in Scotland.

The next project is already under way, with three new stone walls under construction to terrace a steep hill to the side of the barn. I am dreaming about filling this space with hot colors, but am still paralyzed by indecision and covetousness for too many plants.

Last year, I took a sabbatical from my professional life and was lucky enough to persuade Rosemary Verey to allow me to work in her magical garden for a month. That special experience fuelled the fires of my love for my secret garden.

BARBARA ROBINSON, WASHINGTON, CONNECTICUT

XXXIX

A Tangle of Flowering Spaces

> *In Radnorshire – in a valley of patchwork fields and oak woods six hundred feet above sea-level – there is a secret garden within a secret garden. If you ask directions in the nearby village, few people could point the way. It cannot be seen from any road, and only in winter, from one of the surrounding hills, with powerful binoculars trained on its four acres, will you detect a nebula of evergreen hedges and a few majestic trees among the seemingly random cross-stitch of bridle paths and lanes.'*

In ANCIENT TIMES, when map-makers were confronted with a land of which they knew nothing, they were inclined to write, rather poetically, 'here be dragons'. This fearsome creature, symbol of Wales, could still be thought to be in residence, for to many people the principality is regarded as a mysterious place, shrouded in mists and unwelcoming to visitors. It is also believed that there are no gardens in Wales – this despite three of Britain's finest being within its borders. One is tempted to write across horticultural maps which continue to draw a blank west of Herefordshire, 'here be gardens'.

The heart of Wales, an area of deep river valleys and barren moorland, of dense forest and bleak mountainside, is at first sight unlikely gardening country. The winters are undeniably long, cold and wet, with average rainfalls sometimes reaching seventy inches in the Brecon Beacons.

In Radnorshire – in a valley of patchwork fields and oak woods six hundred feet above sea-level – there is a secret garden within a secret garden. If you ask directions in the nearby village, few people could point the way. It cannot be seen from any road, and only in winter, from one of the surrounding hills, with powerful binoculars trained on its four acres, will you detect a nebula of evergreen hedges and a few majestic trees among the seemingly random cross-stitch of bridle paths and lanes.

The Neuadd (pronounced Noy-uth or Ny-uth, and meaning The Hall) lies on the banks of the Elan River near Rhayader. It is tucked below a wooded bank to the east and protected from the furious westerlies by riverside alders and willows. To reach its gates you must pursue a rough stone-strewn track that seems to stop at a farm. But beyond the farmyard, with its raucous company of geese and sheepdogs eager to chase any passers-by, there is the first glimpse of bristling topiary behind gates with piers surmounted by mischievous-looking gargoyles.

In the ninth century there was a monastery here, but seen today the house, with additions still being made, is of the early 1800s. Much of the existing garden layout dates from this period, although extensive work done in the years flanking the First World War has given the place an unmistakably Edwardian atmosphere.

When I discovered the property in 1987 I soon detected among decades of undergrowth such tell-tale signs as a rose garden with a sundial set in a millstone, and dry-stone walls with flights of steps *à la* Jekyll and Lutyens. Years before, on flat ground immediately in front of the house, someone had begun to break the area into a series of outdoor 'rooms', although the long runs of yew and box hedges no more than hint at this ambitious scheme.

Within a few months of moving to The Neuadd, I was joined by artist Simon Dorrell. Together we have learned many of the garden's secrets (one concerning buried sculptures in the orchard) and have given ourselves an ambitious plan, adopting as our motto Shakespeare's line, 'In delay there lies no plenty'.

By country-house standards the garden is not large. Its wealth lies in its contours and natural features: surrounding the detailed formality of terrace, lawns and topiary are streams, former paddocks and steeply rising hillsides. Whatever the conditions, swirling mists, sheeting rain or Mediterranean-like sunshine filtering through giant Scots pines, it is impossible not to feel the romance of the place its garden embedded within the wider landscape.

Recognizing this romantic quality, we have embarked upon a new adventure, not only to restore what was already there but to create for ourselves a mannerist garden with magpie borrowings from centuries of English and European garden ideas.

Hidden somewhere in the new ordered tangle of flowery spaces defined with row upon row of yew, box or beech

ABOVE: 'A Mannerist garden with magpie borrowings'. In the herb garden, Simon Dorrell's four ochre-washed obelisks are complemented by box bushes clipped to the same shape. Culinary herbs grow among foxgloves and pinks in sixteen triangular beds. RIGHT: He also designed the fourteen-foot columns crowned by musicians. The Edwardian sundial has sage, alchemilla, roses and peonies.

hedges, there is one particular enclosure, small and rectangular, where 'Paul's Himalayan Musk' rose swings lazily from the branches of an old English yew: the secret garden, smallest of the nesting dolls. It shines through the seasons, white tulips followed by white martagon lilies, white-edged glossy hostas, chalky-coloured Japanese anemones and spikes of pale verbascum. This secret garden reveals itself only to the most inquisitive of eyes. The feeling of confinement on warm sunny days is strangely comforting and flower scents seem trapped for all time.

The idea of a secret garden – the *hortus conclusus* as it was known in medieval times, the *giardino segreto* beloved of the Italians down the ages – has an even stronger hold on present-day gardeners, like Simon and myself, who hanker for a private refuge in an ever-filling world.

DAVID WHEELER, RHAYADER, POWYS

XL

A Paradise from many Lands

A plantswoman's sure touch – structured height and massing.

Anyone passing by this garden will see a brick wall, four light posts, two gates, a circular driveway, boundary hedges, a house, a lawn, and plantings of evergreens and groundcovers. Access is, by design, neither inviting nor forbidding, just neutral, with no hint of the garden that lurks behind the house. But if you come through the gate and continue under the brick arch and along the garage wall, under the sorbaria tunnel, you will encounter a world of lemon trees, vines, flowering shrubs, and towering and sprawling perennials. Here also dwell screeching squirrels, obnoxious blue jays, begging goldfish and lots of insects. 'Controlled chaos', my friend George Waters once called it, and he's right, and I like it that way.

Visitors seem either to respond enthusiastically to this flouncy world, especially if given a cool drink and excused from participation in my ongoing chore, or they become quiet and mystified, even frightened. Perhaps this is part of my secret – that I can deal with the garden efficiently, and love the excitement and change naturally created by an environment where plants, animals and insects are allowed freely to flourish. I even accept, quite happily, the disasters nature deals us, such as ice storms, volcanoes, droughts, realizing that it only means another great change.

The first thing I did on my arrival here was to install a six-foot brown

A dramatic transition from the tranquillity of lawn to the activity of perennials in the pond garden. Through the arch of *R.* 'Old Dawson Rose', guarded on one side by foxgloves and variegated box, on the other by laurel and hostas, a different world is revealed. A pot of lustrous-leaved *Agapanthus africanus* is set against furry grey stachys, and purple *Campanula muralis* grows over the narrow path.

board fence around four sides of the property, announcing and marking my territory, not unlike an animal in the woods. Then I added the front gates of friendly curved metal and two wooden gates at the rear. Inside these I began to build my idea of paradise, drawn from the places I visit – a little Italy, a lot of England and France, some Morocco/Spain, and India, which I can't yet figure out how to incorporate.

I believe in boundaries, barriers, physical and psychological, separating us from the world in general. Gates, for example, give or make reason to pause before entry, preparing one for the beyond – a nice thing. They are like membranes that let mostly beneficial particles through. Beneficial in my territory means friends, invited strangers, helpers, almost anyone bearing gifts or boxes, a bottle of wine or good news. Certain animals and insects manage to enter from the air or underground. They get several chances to adjust to my rules before traps or non-poisonous discipline is administered. Early in my life here a weasel took the chickens' eggs, but housing projects did him in, and the pheasants too. Racoons try to eat my fish, but I have made the pond purposely too deep, so they mangle the pots of water plants instead of catching fish. Squirrels live in the heaps of wood, in old containers and often in my attic, and a hawk or two has managed to survive our human overpopulation.

When in 1972 I moved to this old house that had been built forty years earlier by an Englishman and his Scottish wife, I found a deliciously derelict three-quarters of an acre to attack. It was filled with old, large fruit and nut trees, shrubs, a rumpled lawn, a falling-down shed, a greenhouse with no glass and a cottonwood tree growing in the floor. You can imagine my excitement at the challenge.

The plot is very oddly shaped, with five non-parallel sides, situated on a south-facing slope of acid clay. The shape adds to the magic and mystery of the garden, though it was hard to cope with at first. I used the lines of the house, working outwards, to make some sense, leaving some old trees and shrubs as focal points and visual barriers. In trying to get from house to shed to corners, the paths had to take odd turns to compensate for the angles. I feel that it is somewhat successful when I find momentarily lost and happily confused visitors wandering around. And, because of the visual barriers, the property seems bigger than it really is. Peeking over, under, around and through plants or structures creates surprises and new perspectives. Perhaps I'm more aware of these things because, as a garden photographer, I've had to make magic out of too many neat and tidy, boring gardens.

I was lucky to have big brothers with chainsaws and talents with brick and cement. Then they were creative and long-

Misty in early autumn, the end of the long walk narrows to make the vista appear still longer; *Yucca glauca* is the focal point. The repetition of box balls, agapanthus foxgloves and *Hosta plantaginea* binds the composition, and the untamed exuberance of perovskia and *Nicotiana sylvestris* within the shelter of boundary trees give this part of the garden the atmosphere of a woodland glade.

suffering, but you won't see them here now in their workclothes. We removed the horizontal lilac from the shed roof, replaced windows, introduced water, put a top on the greenhouse, added a chicken and rabbit pen (which later became a proper lathhouse with a finch aviary) connected to a terrace with a pond, fish, bubbling fountain for sound, all under an old tree for shade. On a hot day this is my little Spanish spot.

In two corners, carved out of overgrown shrubbery, are hidden work areas with compost piles, stashes of treasure only a gardener would collect. Not beautiful in some people's eyes, to me divine. Squatting by a huge rotting compost heap, dividing plants in the warm March sun with fragrant viburnum scenting the air, screaming blues jays looking for romance and squirrels gone mad because I'm here again – heaven, and not unlike England.

Later in the summer, July-August, when I'm exhausted from staking, watering or life in general, I simply lie down on the grass between two throbbing perennial beds under an old pear tree dangling with heavy ripening Bosch fruits – Eden. Great perspective and a great place for a quick nap. I've done it for years.

But my favorite, and most private, spot is the herb terrace, situated in a south-facing corner between two walls. It's warm

Looking along the long walk in the other direction, towards the pond terrace, the Bloom border on the left is named after the great plantsman Alan Bloom. In front of the mushroom cloud of *Crambe cordifolia*, iris and foxgloves rise above a mixture of rounded and feathery foliage, punctuated by clipped dwarf box. A purple-leaved prunus hangs over the pond and lath-house making this a cool place to sit.

even in winter, and I can grow tender things here. With eight lemon pots producing nicely, it's Italy. This terrace is really about food, fragrance, birds and bees – I plant with them all in mind. There is a wonderful little humming-bird that returns yearly, and if I sit with my head in a honeysuckle vine, he will hover very close, the nearest I've come to feeling like a flower.

When the deciduous trees and shrubs are full and the perennials at their tallest, and I can't see any neighbors' houses, I feel as if secrets can be made and kept here. I can dream and scheme, then share with the world, if I want to. How could this be done without an enclosure? Hiding beauty from the world at large may sound selfish, but gardens are an extension of our houses and selves, and as the world crowds in we need a private place to feed our souls, or just plain hide.

CYNTHIA WOODYARD, PORTLAND, OREGON

NATURAL GARDENS

I'll walk where my own nature would be leading –
It vexes me to choose another guide –
Where the grey flocks in ferny glens are feeding,
Where the wild wind blows on the mountain-side.

Emily Brontë (1818–1848): Untitled

XLI

VILLAGE SECRET

Lustrous, wild, yellow kingcups flourish at the water's edge.

THE LYDE GARDEN came about partly by accident and partly by design. Over the centuries some fifteen springs from the top of the Chilterns have scoured away a deep ravine, or chine, from the surrounding chalk. These springs are the source of the small River Lyde, which eventually joins the River Thame and the River Thames. For a century or so, the springs have formed a series of watercress beds surrounded by magnificent wych-elms. A small path leads down to the ponds from the road near the eleventh-century church – itself only ten feet or so away from the chalk cliff.

There is an old village saw which goes: 'Those who live and do abide shall see Bledlow church fall in the Lyde.' We very much hope not, and have done our best with planting and revetting to see that it does not happen – at any rate, in our lifetime.

In the early 1970s elm disease killed all the trees, leaving a wilderness of brambles and elder, nettles and ash saplings. We decided in 1979 to try and make a garden to replace this unsightly and desolate wilderness. It was not just to be our garden, but a village garden, open to all who wanted to see or sit in it.

We called in Robert Adams, a landscape architect and a friend, who had helped us previously with the garden round our house, and together we discussed what should be done. His expertise, enthusiasm and knowledge were the turning point for what at first seemed a rather dubious enterprise. We discussed a number of options, but decided to keep the existing steep contours untouched as far as possible, whilst making paths and channelling some of the spring water into a small pond, with a course running down to what was then the watercress bed.

The first thing to do was to clear the mess. That was the only time we thought we might have made the most appalling mistake. When cleared, the area looked exactly as if it had been prepared for excavation by the local cement works – a white desert. It seemed impossible that anything, even the toughest and bravest of weeds, could possibly grow on the unappetizing soil we had uncovered. Mutterings were reported to us from neighbours in the village. They thought not only that we had gone mad but that we had ruined a rather attractive wild area to which we had all become accustomed and which anyway could not be seen. But the die was cast.

We gritted our teeth and started planting. We decided to leave the western side, which was marshy, until later, and tackle the eastern side, which was a dry bank, first. We chose a variety of species plants, which we hoped would grow in the unpromising environment. Planting itself was quite difficult since the cliff-like sides of the ravine were very steep.

We used a lot of *Sorbaria kirilowii*

Tucked away out of sight, this natural garden is at the heart of a little-known English village. Hidden in a ravine just below the church, it is lined with a series of spring-fed ponds. In 1979 the unsightly, desolate and overgrown wilderness it had become was cleared; now mallard and moorhen use the aviary eye-catcher, and hostas, astilbes, *Primula florindae* and day-lilies have colonized at the water's edge.

arborea, which produces beautiful white panicles of fluffy flowers in August, but are turned all too soon dispiritingly brown by a heavy fall of rain. *Euonymus europaeus*, *Viburnum opulus* and *Elaeagnus angustifolia* grow well. So do *Hippophaë rhamnoides*, *Corylus laciniata* 'Purpurea', various cotoneasters and berberis and *Colutea arborescens*. *Prunus lusitanica* and *P. laurocerasus* supply the form and philadelphus the scent. Alnus, sorbus, betula, mespilus, prunus and pyrus grow among species roses, which have to hold their own amongst their vigorous neighbours. We brought an ailanthus seedling from London – supposedly a lime hater, it has grown to ten metres in ten years.

When it was finished, the east bank still looked exactly like the cement works with a few twigs inserted here and there and a long way apart. To our astonishment, in a very short time the planting took hold and masked the paths. The geranium, vinca and symphytum we brought down to cover the chalk spread miraculously, and the criticisms were to some extent stilled. Today our problem is too vigorous growth.

Emboldened, we decided to tackle the wet half. Robert designed a walkway made of hardwood from Ghana and two bridges across what was still the watercress bed. These, he assured us, would last for ever since the timber had been soaked in sea water for two years.

A simple rustic wooden bridge and steps – made from Ghanaian hardwood soaked in sea water for two years – give the garden a semi-Asiatic character. Willow trees overhanging clumps of kingcup and a host of other water-loving plants lie at the bottom of the ravine. Looking down from on high, the spectacle is one of a mass of lush foliage crossing three converging chalk springs.

Next we attacked the watercress. Children, grandchildren and guests, willing and unwilling, were dragooned into grubbing it up. Those who have tried to do this will know that, though you may appear to have been successful, it is only a very short time before the watercress re-appears. To this day we are still plagued with it, though optimistically we believe that every time is the last.

The marshy bits were planted with gunneras, darmera, ferns, bamboo, astilbes, hostas, primulas, dodecatheon, caltha and hemerocallis amidst what has turned out to be the most persistent, vigorous and obstinate creeping buttercup known to man. On the slopes we planted salix, aralia and cornus which thrive amongst the existing sycamore saplings.

For a time you could still look down from the road and see the whole garden laid out before you. Now nothing can be seen, and until you reach the bottom there is no indication that there is water or a bridge or a garden.

The *Metasequoia glyptostroboides* have grown into fine trees. We have planted swamp cypress, cut-leaf alder, *Hydrangea sargentiana* and two golden poplars. *Cornus alba* 'Elegantissima' draws the eye across the water, and iris – *I. laevigata*, *ensata* (*kaempferi*), *pseudacorus* and *sibirica* – inulas, ligularia, lysimachia and lysichiton have found damp or wet conditions to suit their needs.

The springs have never dried up, even in these last drought-ridden years. The old ram, which used to be the only water supply for the house 150 feet above it, still works. The three watercress beds are now three separate ponds on different levels - none of them planted. The clear water reflects the foliage around it, the weeping willows, the irises, the grasses, the two bridges and the ever-changing sky.

In the middle of the upper pond we have placed a small white aviary (which we saw at Christie's and which was originally intended for a garden, not, as some think, for the birds to nest in – it is far too public), which gives the garden

The walkway leads from the dry eastern side of the valley over many springs which are the source of the little River Lyde. The three present ponds were once watercress beds. A profusion of garden flowers occurs here in a wild water setting: *Geranium* 'Johnson's Blue', *Senecio* 'Sunshine', ligularia and day-lilies, backed by golden variegated cornus. Unseen by passers-by, the garden is known only to villagers and enthusiasts.

and its bridges a slightly Japanese look. The bird population has greatly increased in variety and we are now privileged to have a kingfisher.

In a way it is wrong to call it a secret garden since it is enjoyed and visited by an increasing number of appreciative people, who are both tidy and thoughtful. But they and we think of it as secret since it is hidden away. Children love it, adults enjoy it, lovers court in it. It enchants us because it is so very different from the gardens around the house, and also because we are vain enough to think we have created something a little unusual, partly by accident and with a lot of help.

LORD CARRINGTON, BLEDLOW, BUCKINGHAMSHIRE

XLII

A MOUNTAIN EYRIE

Yellow laburnum and purple centaurea – a classic confrontation.

I CAME HOME TO WALES twenty years ago when I bought a remote and dilapidated farmhouse nestling in the Berwyn mountains. It was one of those golden September days, the hills purple with heather, rowan trees full of berry. We found the house up a steep, narrow lane, and I knew immediately that this could be home. It brought back so many memories of my childhood in Wales. Friends were pessimistic, seeing only an isolated house in need of total renovation and a garden non-existent except for a box hedge, one climbing rose and man-high weeds.

Where to begin? While architect and builders started on the house, the garden became my obsession. Out came a hawthorn hedge, to reveal the mountains hanging with mist and a natural ha-ha giving the impression that the sheep were grazing in the garden. A stream ran underground at the front of the house – when we moved tons of soil to form a flat area onto which the roofing slates taken off the roof could be stacked, we could see the stream rushing over boulders of granite.

Boulders are literally the backbone of Dolwen; I found that I was on the site of an ice age glacier. They have dictated the shape of the flower beds, and where to plant trees: no use deciding on the perfect place for something, then crashing the spade into solid granite. Their enormous advantage is that plants love to get their toes under them, and

At Dolwen the wider landscape and the mountains are inescapably part of the garden, as are the twin elements of water and stone. The edge of the lower pond is fringed with foliage plants – ligularia, bronze *Darmera peltata* and hostas. Pink foxgloves, purple and yellow iris and white *Rosa* 'Nevada' add brighter touches to the relaxed medley of colour among the restful green of lawn and leaves.

the grey colouring complements the flowers, especially pink shrub roses and lime-green *Helleborus argutifolius* (syn. *H. corsicus*). Local slate has been used in many forms – broken up to make paths, large slabs for bridges, even small pieces of roofing slate written on in oil pencil as plant labels.

The small garden was soon overflowing with cottage-garden plants: peonies, aquilegias, roses, clematis and poppies galore. Walls were hung with honeysuckle, ceanothus and more roses; we even had a tiny vegetable patch. Life was too good to be true, then Oliver died and I badly needed something to fill my life again.

In a fit of wild optimism, I bought the adjoining four acres of land and some derelict outbuildings. Round and round I walked that winter in thick snow, falling over boulders, falling into the bog. What could I possibly do to make an alder copse, bramble scrub and a wet, two-acre field into a garden?

The stream running the whole length was obviously going to be the life-giving energy of the garden. With the help of the first of my two enthusiastic and brawny helpers, I moved stones to form pools, with small falls of water to increase the sound. I was back to my childhood. The first winter taught me a hard lesson, for mountain streams have a mind of their own, and storms turned the water into a roaring torrent, sweeping away precious plants.

Boulders, worn smooth over centuries, are the back-bone of the garden. PREVIOUS PAGE: Looking down from one of the slate bridges, a nymph vies for attention with huge stones among stream-moistened foliage. In the foreground, *Smilacina racemosa* is in flower. RIGHT: Grey boulders, piled high, provide a perfect backdrop to delicate shade-loving plants on the walk up to the ponds and stone bridge.

The alder copse was thinned and drained to make huge beds for moisture-loving plants. Rodgersias, ligularias, thalictrum, darmera are now growing to jungle proportions – then suddenly round a corner primulas are clustered in profusion. Curving paths lead one round to cross bridges and catch views of the mountains.

A friendly JCB solved the field problem. Three large ponds, fed by the stream and underground springs, were excavated, and giant boulders – Henry Moore sculptures – came out of the craters. Now the fun began. Luckily I had become a plantaholic and knew vaguely what to grow. I wanted each pond to have its own identity. The first, with a backing of subsoil twelve feet high and an island in the middle, is invaluable as a fox-free haven for ducks; a weeping willow gives extra protection from magpies. Three sides are thickly planted with hostas, gunnera, grasses, swamp cypress and willows, all reflecting in the water, a perfect home for dragonflies. Flat slabs of granite bring water down in a cascade from the second pond, sparsely planted with choice willows, silver pear and *Cornus controversa*. The third is backed by a large curved bed of autumn-coloured shrubs and a high beech hedge on the boundary.

Woodland is growing up slowly on the lane side of the ponds to hide them from the occasional car or tractor. Ginkgo, liquidambar, golden ash, *Prunus serrula*, scarlet oak and various sorbus will eventually make a colourful curtain, underplanted with daffodils.

Every day I walk up the garden to feed my family of ducks, a constant delight as they quack away, playing in the water and eating all the slugs. There is always a big decision to make – which of the four routes to take? Over the curved bridge, up the steps and round the copse; maybe across the lawn to the aged alder, and over the stream to see how the primulas are coming on; or, how about walking past the herbaceous border to pull out a few weeds? No, today I will go through the vegetable garden and plan my dinner. Gardening is much akin to cooking: give two people the same ingredients, the results are never identical.

Like cooking, the seasons bring fresh delights to make me wonder about my favourite flower. The first snowdrops I treasure, so brave to pop up in their hundreds on snow-covered banks. As the seasons change, I have other passions. Poppies must take pride of place; there are so many beauties in the family. First to flower is *Papaver* 'Fireball', a miniature red oriental, which spreads like wildfire. Welsh poppy pops up everywhere in a splash of yellow, with its cousin the double orange. Experts tend to shun the ordinary red oriental; I grow it mixed with *Euphorbia* 'Fireglow', so that the red of the poppy picks up the scarlet theme. The soft pink, feminine 'Mrs Perry' has to be kept well away from 'Beauty of Liver-mere', the colour of a guardsman's tunic. Hylomecon, a Japanese wood poppy, loves my wet woodlands; and then there is the annual 'Fairy Wings', hand-painted in soft pinks and greys.

I must have peonies, too, full of promise from the time their fat buds appear until their short-lived burst of glory. *Paeonia mlokosewitschii*, commonly known as Molly the Witch, flowers for one short week, the colour of Welsh butter. If I could paint I would try to capture my beautiful white tree peony, rightly named 'Ballerina', as her twelve-inch gossamer heads dance across the garden stage.

Shrub roses have found their place on the clay subsoil from the ponds, helped by lashings of manure. *R.* 'Nevada', 'Chianti', 'Constance Spry' and 'Fantin-Latour' light up the shadow cast by tall alders. 'Kiftsgate' is romping away on an old tree, with 'Rambling Rector' trying hard to catch her; as an incentive I have given him 'Wedding Day' for company. The drooping pink 'Raubritter' falls over boulders, and 'Canary Bird', eight feet across, drapes her yellow across the stream.

My dream garden of twenty years ago has gradually taken shape, and now an astonishing spectrum of plants grow in this mountain eyrie 1000 feet up in the Berwyn Mountains.

FRANCES DENBY, CEFN COCH, WELSH BORDERS

XLIII

THROUGH A HOLE IN THE WALL

Plantsman's world: seedlings raised from six show auriculas.

I CAN REMEMBER when I first started gardening. I must have been about six years old. I was brought up by my grandmother, and she went to visit an old lady who was splitting a herbaceous border. I asked if I could have some bits – asters, Shasta daisies – to put into the little patch of garden my grandfather had given me. I've been a gardener ever since, and I'm eighty-seven now.

I started work in a big private garden – pretty much *The Victorian Country Garden* in miniature – a beautiful place, with a rose garden, peacocks and a walled vegetable garden with fruit all the way round. My last job before I retired was as gardener at the Officers' Mess at RAF Spitalgate, near Grantham. I had about five acres to look after, with twenty frames and three biggish greenhouses. I used to grow chiefly bedding plants – thousands of them.

We came to live here in 1955, when we moved from the outskirts of Grantham after my wife had a breakdown in her health. We had to walk up the lane, climb through a hole in the wall and literally push our way through the undergrowth to get to the house. Once a gamekeeper's cottage, it was absolutely derelict, especially inside. An old couple had lived here before and hadn't really bothered about it at all – we had to burn special candles to get rid of the fleas and the lice. The garden was just a sea of docks, elder bushes, nettles and wild-rose briars. I knew what we were up against, but thought we could make something of the place, even though it was in such a mess.

First of all I marked out the big lawn, then planted a lonicera hedge at the back and made a rockery along the side. On the other side I put a herbaceous border, which is still there. If I started again, I wouldn't change the design, except for making my paths wider and planting fewer conifers – I put them in for quick results. The only trees here when we came were a lilac, a May tree and a Portugal laurel.

I planted the garden more or less as I went along, putting the plants where they would be most suited. I'm not afraid of mixing plants – as a rule they don't fall out with one another. There is no particular colour scheme. In the round beds by the house I put a bit of bedding stuff; nowadays that's all the bedding I do, apart from busy lizzies, begonias and a few antirrhinums in pots. I don't like all these annuals: after they are finished, you are left with nothing, while there is always something in flower in my garden all through the year. I have over 2000 varieties of plants, but there are many I can't put a name to.

The old gamekeeper's cottage, its red-brick front covered with 'Goldheart' ivy, is buried in the heart of a hanging wood. Conifers were planted for much-needed protection from bleak westerly winds; the forty-year-old *Cedrus libani atlantica* 'Glauca' was a silver wedding present. In the foreground, hellebores mingle with spring bulbs in a bed dominated by *Erica* 'Arthur Johnson'.

The first shrub to come out is *Cornus mas*, with beautiful little yellow flowers, after the scented *Mahonia* 'Charity' and *Viburnum farreri*, which flower in late winter. I love my fragrant shrubs, especially

The path beside the house is flanked by *Hydrangea macrophylla*, alchemilla and day-lilies in pots. The substantial bulk of a chamaecyparis, raised from a cutting, bars the way into the wood, which gives welcome shelter but lets loose marauding bands of pheasants, squirrels, rabbits, voles and mice. Thousands of snowdrops from the wood have naturalized in the garden.

the daphnes, and I grow caraway seed, thyme, apple mint, eau-de-Cologne mint and lemon balm at different places on the corners of paths, so if I was blindfolded I think I could find my way around just by scent.

Then of course I have thousands of snowdrops – dug out of the wood behind the house. I particularly like species crocus; you get so many delicate colours. I grow miniature daffodils and dwarf tulips, but only in pots indoors – I'm not risking them in the garden any more since the pheasants ate the lot. In the winter they used to come and look in at the back door!

The garden gradually goes from spring bulbs and flowers to herbaceous. I grow a lot of *Erysimum* 'Bowles' Mauve', which flowers for ages, irises, phlox, *Dahlia* 'Bishop of Llandaff', then chrysanthemums and Michaelmas daisies. On the rockery side I've got Bowles' one-leaf strawberry, which they tell me is donkey's years old, a double-flowered strawberry, a green-flowered variety, and a pink-flowered one called 'Pink Panda'. I grow four different sorts of celandine, including a double green, another called 'Brazen Hussy', which is brilliant orange with dark foliage, and a lemony-coloured one.

I like ferns and they do well for me – the lady fern and the hare's foot, and one that came in from the wood but has an unusual cristate end to it. My favourite flower is the lily-of-the-valley, the ordinary white one, although I have the pink-flowered variety too, which has gone mad in the rockery. Cactus interest me; an old fellow left me his collection when he died, so there are some here which are over sixty years old. Best of all I like the alpines, because they are so small and delicate and there are so many different varieties. I became interested in them over fifty years ago.

Spring is my favourite time. In the winter when the place is covered with snow I give up like everybody else. It's very bleak here because, although the garden is sheltered on the north, south and east sides, the wind comes mainly from the west. I am lucky to have the wood as a backdrop behind, protecting the garden and especially the greenhouses; the base of the first one is all rotten, yet it feels as solid as a rock in spite of the shocking gales.

The wood can cause problems, though. The sycamore trees drop awful sticky stuff onto the borders, and, apart from the pheasants, squirrels come in and pinch all the nuts from the copper-leaf nut tree and the corkscrew hazel; and I get rabbits, shrews, voles, and dozens of mice.

A lot of different birds come to the garden – nuthatches, jays, tree creepers, blue tits, long-tailed tits, flycatchers – as well as the bees and butterflies. I've seen peacock butterflies, red admirals, sulphur-coloured ones in spring, cottage whites, even one or two hummingbird hawk moths; they dart around in the most fantastic way and their tongues look about three inches long.

Once I had quite a big vegetable patch down at the bottom of the garden, but the land is more or less solid clay there (although not as bad as our old garden in Grantham, where you could skate on the soil in winter and in a dry summer you could get your legs down the cracks), so these days I go for the easy life and buy what I need. Especially since my wife died – she used to be in service as a cook, so she liked having fresh vegetables. Now I'm alone up here, which I don't mind when I can get out into the garden. The worst part of it is in the winter when I have to sit in the house on my own.

Everybody calls this a secret garden. They come off the road, come in here through the gate and up the path, and say it's a different world, a hidden paradise. I don't know quite how it's become that. I like all things in nature, I suppose that's what it boils down to.

HERBERT EXTON, SYSTON, LINCOLNSHIRE

XLIV

THE CROSSING HOUSE GARDEN

A London-bound train speeds by a trackside strewn with wild flowers.

VISITORS TO OUR SMALL GARDEN may easily mistake the path leading between the greenhouses for the way to a service area, but those who explore further are rewarded by the discovery of a sheltered seat from which to view our secret garden. Not only secret, but also forbidden, for these twin borders, stretching as far as the eye can see, flank the busy Cambridge-to-King's Cross railway line.

A locked gate prevents visitors from trespassing onto property which belongs to British Rail and is very dangerous, so they must view it from a distance – or take a seat on one of the frequent trains and catch a fleeting glimpse, as the train rushes past, of floriferous borders and a knot garden, with terraces and seats rising out of the vegetation and busts staring out from the bushes. In the distance, pampas grass, broom, teasel and rosebay willowherb stand out from a host of cultivated and wild plants, and patches of bindweed, twitch, nettles and brambles. Piles of bricks lie about, waiting to be laid. Here and there are heaps of British Rail debris: rusty wire, chunks of concrete, fencing posts, disused sleepers, ivy-swathed telegraph poles and broken bottles lying where I have collected them, ready to be covered with compost and planted over.

To me, the garden reveals its secrets most in the hushed dawn hours of high summer when, accompanied by a mug of tea, I battle

A warning notice beside the crossing is all but hidden by an exuberant mass of wild red poppies, white matricaria and blue hyssop, with purple lavatera, yellow verbascum and silver-leaved onorpodum in the background. Seedlings collected from any source grow where they please – wild and cultivated plants, birds, animals and insects share the same lovingly tended habitat, liberated from disuse.

sleepily with the weeds before the heat of day brings out hordes of biting ants and flies. Looking up from unravelling goosegrass from larkspur and marigold, I am sometimes rewarded by the sight of foxes strolling across the track. Muntjak deer ignore me despite my high-visibility, BR-issue orange waistcoat. Rabbits nibble at the vegetation – no problem to me as there is plenty of greenery for all.

As the sun comes up, cuckoos, blackbirds and pigeons fill the air with a deafening chorus of welcome to the new day. When the warmth of the sun has driven away the early morning dew, lizards scuttle out from hiding places and bask in the heat on the wooden sides of a redundant chippings bin, filled now with peat and surplus calcifuge plants. Grasshoppers chirp cheerfully on the dry banks and ladybirds decorate plants like mobile jewels. Birds feed on the bounty: a flycatcher sits on his favourite fence post with a beakful of breakfast, a jay dazzles my eyes and skylarks carol merrily over the nearby fields.

Six foot of angelica suddenly rears up out of the blue geranium. A self-sown gooseberry bush provides light refreshment. Pennyroyal, mint and southernwood perfume the air as they are trampled underfoot. Old-fashioned roses claw my clothing and humming bees carpet the purple thyme flowers. A myriad of seedlings jostles for light

and space, bindweed thugging its way to the top, a giant grey thistle flattening competition over a square yard and reaching for the sky. The godetia needs thinning, and heavenly scented white alyssum rampages over the dry, dusty margin of a steep bank, where little else seems to flourish except for stonecrop, pinks and rock roses.

Weeding the borders is never dull – although I planted them myself, I have no idea what I am going to find next. Packets of 'Lottery Mix' seed and unnamed donations of plants and seeds from generous garden visitors ensure never-ending surprises.

Small shrubs – cotoneaster, sage, the curry plant, rue and potentilla – form the backbone of the planting, and throughout the year I gather armloads of seedling alliums, hellebores, hollyhocks and mallows and toss them along the borders – an untidy but quick way to spread them over a large area. Rather than eliminate the native plants, the more ornamental ones have been encouraged to carry on the good work of decorating the countryside. Hawthorn has been clipped into neat shapes; buttercup, speedwell, ground ivy, red deadnettle and the yellow shaving brushes of the coltsfoot are welcome in the spring. Scarlet poppies intermarry with

Alongside the unlikely setting of the Cambridge-to-London line, where the crossing keeper's hut faces the crossing house, double Shirley poppies and *Papaver somniferum* cluster thickly with blue larkspur. Sadly, the trackside garden has now been ruled out of bounds to its self-appointed curators by railway officials, and weeds are already taking over from the beauty of the transient flowers.

the shirleys; lemon-yellow linaria, white campion and wild scabious fill gaps; and wild roses can be counted on to furnish the garden with a brilliant display of scarlet hips for much of the autumn and early winter. Bulbs are in their element and I am constantly dividing and replanting. Snowdrops and snowflakes relish the dry conditions, daffodils multiply and the huge red tulips I find overpowering at close quarters make a cheerful splash of colour in the distance.

In winter toads come to hibernate and bury themselves in decaying vegetation, grandfathers and little ones, to be carefully avoided by the digging fork. Then magic pervades the garden. Freezing fog creates a fairyland. Brown clumps of Michaelmas daisies and shrubs are wrapped in a sparkling shroud of glittering hoar frost laced with encrusted spiders' webs, and the borders loom in and out of sight as the fog drifts down the track. The sound of the trains is muffled to a murmur; even the missel thrush is silenced.

Perhaps the secret of the garden's sorcery is its very lack of permanence. At the moment I have lost the battle with the weeds and the borders are reverting to a wilderness, as British Rail has given me my marching orders.

Margaret Fuller, Shepreth, Cambridgeshire

XLV

THE VALLEY AND THE WATERFALL

Eye-catching hosta leaves overhung by giant fans of gunnera.

I N 1959 Sarah and I were living in Calne, close to our work as agriculturists. We wanted to separate the two, and resolved to find a small Georgian or William and Mary house a short distance away. As suitable properties, on a good site and in a state of repair commensurate with our income did not appear to exist, we resolved to build, lending force to the old saying that 'fools build houses and wise men live in them'.

Finding a site was almost as difficult: even in 1959 the planning authorities took rather a poor view of those who wished to make extensive gardens instead of choosing to live in high-rise blocks or on housing estates. One day when we were motoring just west of Devizes, Sarah noticed a minor road called Conscience's Lane, leading across to the Chippenham road. This road separated the downland chalk, upon which the Battle of Roundway Down took place in 1642, from the upper greensand to the south.

Here we found thirty-three acres of mixed ancient woodland forming part of the old Roundway estate. The grand dwelling occupied by the Colston family (who made their fortune from the slave trade) had been demolished soon after the 1939-45 war and part of the stable block converted into an elegant house. The estate was then bought by the Merchant Venturers, the ancient charitable trust based in Bristol.

After prolonged negotiations the trust refused to sell us an individual site but said that if we would take the complete woodland, which had become a management problem, they would be inclined to sell. I spent some months measuring and

pricing the timber and put in a modest bid; this was advertised, as required by law, in an obscure newspaper which seemed to command few readers, and was finally accepted.

It was at this stage that our mistakes began – and they continue to this day. We set about thinning the woodland, largely to finance the building of a house, for which we had received planning permission. In fact, of course, the end of collective support meant that a major gale flattened those trees remaining, and the site looked rather like the Ypres salient. After an immense labour of clearing and cleaning, we replanted with 35,000 young trees, in too wide a variety, which had to be weeded regularly for five years; in most cases these are now two-thirds fully grown.

A small dry valley to the west bounds a a six-acre plateau on which the house stands, surrounded by the garden and including a small paddock. A one-acre lawn has views to the south-west; on a really clear day Alfred's Tower may be seen above Stourhead, twenty-five miles away. Herbaceous borders adjoin the lawn on two sides, and roses, clematis and other climbers scramble up walls and over trees. Rhododendrons and camellias can be grown on our marginally acid greensand; after flowering they are sometimes rather dull, so we have interplanted them with a wide range of shrubs, bamboos and grasses.

Curving walks lead towards the eastern edge of the plateau, where steep paths plunge eighty feet into the most secret part of the garden – a valley in which flows a spring-fed stream.

This runs into a small lake, then discharges at the southern end over a twenty-foot waterfall, continuing through the middle water garden and on into the lower garden, where it joins another stream. The joint waters are the most easterly source of the Bristol Avon. The streams are crossed by four bridges, the largest just above the waterfall, the plangent sound of which is constant company. Although it is only just over a mile from the centre of a busy town, the water garden gives an impression of extreme remoteness.

The valley had marvellous natural topography, but it was rapidly succumbing to an aggressive bamboo, *Arundinaria anceps*. Fortunately, and for the first time in living memory, which must be at least seventy years, the whole lot seeded and, as bamboos are monocarpic, promptly died. We were unwise enough to replant a few seedlings, so in time we will discover whether *A. anceps* finally wins.

Primulas abound below and above the falls. Clothing the

ABOVE: A twenty-foot waterfall – almost a Himalayan spectacle – separates the small lake from the middle water garden, flanked by a large clump of *Arundinaria nitida*. RIGHT: Different primulas, including the pink-flowered candelabra *Primula japonica*, among water-loving plants on the banks of the small stream which, fed by two constant springs, maintains its level through the year.

banks of the combined streams are water-loving plants: rodgersias, lysichiton, ligularias, lobelias and large clumps of gunnera – all in considerable diversity of species. On the lower lawn is a small colony of the colourful toothwort, *Lathraea clandestina*, which is parasitic on the roots of willows and poplars. Specimen trees – *Cornus kousa, Halesia monticola, Metasequoia glyptostroboides, Liriodendron chinense, Sorbus wardii, Alnus × spaethii, A. hirsuta* – add interest. Also included is a representative selection of bamboos, while hostas proliferate in between.

Our main interest is the growing, propagation and distribution of rare and threatened plants, vast numbers of which are lost, many before they have even been recorded by taxonomists. On acquiring something new, we try to propagate and give plants away to likely husbandmen; they might not survive in our garden, but in someone else's they will grow like weeds.

JOHN PHILLIPS, HOME COVERT, WILTSHIRE

XLVI

A MISSISSIPPI WATER GARDEN

'Even then, I saw the secret garden among the weeds. That was twenty years ago, and now I've restored the 500-square-foot cabin as my home . . . the garden has evolved just as I pictured in my imagination. It's a stroll garden, the Mississippi version of a water garden.'

WHEN A FRIEND, Janet Redmont, and I set out to find the former slave cabin behind her house, the brush was so thick we almost gave up. We spent two hours getting there, and the saplings had grown so close to the cabin that we couldn't prise open the door. After being abandoned as farmland, the land had grown unchecked for twenty years. There must have been 500 plants per square foot: it was so dense you couldn't see three feet ahead.

Even then, I saw the secret garden among the weeds. That was twenty years ago, and now I've restored the 500-square-foot cabin as my home and the setting for the paintings, pottery, white oak baskets, wood carvings and other crafts collected during fourteen years as director of the Craftsmen's Guild of Mississippi. More important, the garden has evolved just as I pictured in my imagination. It's a stroll garden, the Mississippi version of a Japanese water garden. I laugh because Japanese visitors would probably say it looks like an American garden. Perhaps it would be more accurate if I were to refer to it as a redneck Japanese water garden.

More people than I can count have called it a secret garden since it's hidden away and reached by turning off a two-lane country road on to a gravel driveway. Sitting in the quiet of the garden, you forget about the school a stone's throw away and the new housing developments under

Carved out of dense undergrowth in the Mississippi swampland, the beds facing the old slave cabin are dwarfed by the elongated trunks of thickly clustered trees – sassafras, persimmon and water oak. Their thick canopy keeps the garden several degrees cooler than the surrounding countryside. Light and shadow play over the artfully placed boulders and naturalistic, layered beds.

construction nearby. Strangely enough, I recall *The Secret Garden* as one of the first books I read as a child; even then the sense of place appealed to me.

My home is so small that the garden is like having another room. A tin-roofed porch tacked on to the back of the grey cabin overlooks the yard and is where friends congregate for conversation washed down with iced tea. It's the place I choose most often to spend a leisurely afternoon reading. For sitting, I've got a collection of wooden children's chairs like those you might find at a kindergarten, sturdy, comfortable and easy to move around.

My kitchen window swings open right on to the porch, which allows me to cook inside and converse with visitors outside. Even in the hottest months, the garden is about ten degrees cooler than the land outside because of the surrounding shade trees. I'm probably one of the few people in Mississippi who doesn't have air conditioning.

I started by clearing a five-inch deer trail that wound around the property. Landscape architects would come and compliment me on the sensitive way I would responded to the environment, and I would tell them the deer were my consultants. I'm still paying heavily for their advice: I'll come out and find that they have eaten all my strawberry begonias right down to the ground.

A closer view reveals the subtlety of the planting, relying on the infinite variety of leaf shapes and textures
to create a picture of changing intrigue. Water hyacinths grow in the shallow water beside a mat of lysimachia. Ferns, shrubs and grasses, in a wealth of
shades, create a landscape that is entirely green, save
for the many-coloured leaves of the copper plant.

Next I established the meadows beyond the garden by cutting down thousands of saplings and mowing every four or five days. Actually, that's where and how I learned to garden, by studying the play of light on native plants. Before that, I didn't know better and would invariably put shade plants in the sun and sun-loving plants in the shade.

The beds around my house came last. I resisted the urge to create an English border garden as some visitors suggested – such a garden would be difficult to maintain in Mississippi with its warm summer temperatures and winter frosts. The beds, which run in circles around the house, took form after a garden center delivered three big rocks on a flatbed truck. I made patterns with the rocks and toyed around with those patterns until I found the perfect spots – I knew that once they were in place it would be impossible to move them without a crane. One of those rocks is in the center of the garden, where a canopy of trees opens overhead. In the early morning, that rock is the center of attention; later, the sun shines on a Japanese maple with branches that cascade like a fountain in a raised bed. Then, in the afternoon, the back meadow where the native indigo thrives opens up and the front of the garden returns to shade.

My garden is a green garden, fenced by privet hedges clipped into mushroom shapes or what I call 'cloud bushes', and nandina bushes trimmed into reed-like stalks so that they live up to their Japanese nickname of heavenly bamboo. It is cool and calm, with texture and a touch of colour – red salvia, pink impatiens – but nothing too dominant or overpowering.

From painting classes I learned tricks landscape painters use to create depth. That's why I layered plants in circular patterns, mixing native plants with those from Japan and

paths of stone and rocks. A stream snakes through and adds the soothing sound of water. For interest, there's a Japanese lantern, a fountain and African folk sculpture carved in stone. A gazing ball - a birthday gift from a friend – is surrounded by tin panels that came off the columns at the former state institution for the mentally ill. On the porch, a marble rabbit, carved by a Mississippi craftsman, greets visitors when my cat fails to do the job. Square-shaped planters hold moss and bonsai plants. An iron pot filled with water contains water hyacinths and goldfish, which the racoons sometimes surprise and scoop from the water. A bird feeder filled with seeds and a humming-bird feeder with red-coloured nectar invite cardinals to visit.

As I've grown as a gardener, my life has changed. I retired seven years ago after a car accident, and I would have lost my mind if I hadn't had the garden. When I'm here the world seems much more at ease with itself – perhaps it's the garden's spirit-catching quality. I'm not as strong as I once was, but I'm a better gardener. As I've gotten older and more arthritic, the once mile-long trail has grown shorter. My philosophy is if it hurts or seems like work you're doing it wrong. I've learned to work with nature rather than against it. Almost all the beds are made of composted leaves, partly for convenience, because I couldn't have picked up the leaves and carried them away, partly out of ecological concern. I'll rake leaves and twigs and toss them under the beds. I lie on a blanket and pull weeds. I've got just enough grass so that I can mow with a pushmower. Slowing down physically has made me a better observer and let me allow nature to run its own affairs, helping it along rather than always trying to attack it with a machete or a chainsaw.

DAN OVERLY, RIDGELAND, MISSISSIPPI

XLVII

A LIVING MAXFIELD PARRISH PAINTING

A fountain mask by Dick Rosmini drowns in a sea of plant spawn.

I HAVE A TERRACE in my garden, where we sit at a marble table under a deodar, listen to a trickling fountain, and look out through the trees to a cluster of tile-roofed buildings on a wooded hillside and layers of misty blue hills beyond. Often people who come here say, 'This is magical, this could be any-where in the world! The South of France! This could be Italy!' Well maybe, but it's actually Los Angeles, about ten minutes from City Hall. Those chimes are an ice-cream truck, not the village church, and that's Occidental College across the val-ley, not a ruined abbey, but the magic is indisputable. I can hardly take credit for the view or the golden afternoon light, and the giant Italian cypresses were here long before we came, but this terrace is the heart of the garden, our dining-room and summer livingroom. On the crumbling stucco porch nearby, my husband and I sat twenty years ago – the slightly dazed new owners – and dreamed happily of how the garden should go.

We began with a nicely laid-out tangle sixty or seventy years old at the end of a quiet street: a square half-acre with a tiny stucco house and many beautiful large trees. Neither of us wanted to disturb the feeling of remoteness of this living Maxfield Parrish painting, but we had some grand ideas. I knew I wanted a garden with a strong architectural framework to give a feeling of permanence and repose

Ten minutes from the heart of Los Angeles, the garden is intended to evoke the atmosphere of a grand garden in a state of decay. On the terrace, under the filtering light of a deodar cedar, a mournful, pensive lady is swathed in a feathery full length opera cloak of Spanish moss. Since this photograph was taken, she has been denuded to provide a silver lining to some squirrel's nest.

and allow a generous abandon of planting. I wanted places to grow too many plants, a water garden, and mystery and fra-grance, and I wanted it to look as though it had been that way from the beginning of time. The hillside called for terracing, and the trees would provide the shade necessary in this cli-mate, where gardening is a matter of light and shadow. The lemon trees and the huge *Pittosporum undulatum* would alter-nately drown the place in fragrance, and there would be old roses and old pots with lilies in them, and quite a bit of this eventually came to pass. My good friend Bob Grimes says my garden is trying to give the impression that maybe two hundred years ago this was a really terrific neighborhood.

My Sissinghurst-like fantasies of garden rooms full of color were quickly modified. The reality of a steep north slope with all the big trees at the top put symmetrical formality beyond my resources and sunlight at a premium; romantic melan-choly was going to be easy, a blaze of color was not. This forced me to think of foliage color and form above flower dis-play, and to seek out the mild-climate plants that might per-form well, and variegated plants that would light up dark spaces.

Since I design gardens for other people, it would probably be politic to say this was all carefully planned from the start, but in truth I made it up as I went along and changed directions several times in the pro-

cess. Everything proceeds with geologic slowness because I insist on doing a lot of it myself; my husband offers sensible advice and wisely stays out of the path of the juggernaut.

I began by chopping things out, twenty-foot pyracanthas, suckers from the plum trees bigger than the plum trees, blackberries – everything I needed to take out had ferocious thorns. I built my terraces with drystone walls of scavenged broken concrete sidewalk and granite cobblestones liberated years ago from an abandoned estate. Next to a beautiful S-curve of an existing hedge I laid out a brick path in a pattern of interlocking fan shapes; this joins a wide terrace path that runs below the house and links it to other parts of the garden. Above the path I put a bed for shade-tolerant perennials and on the other side of the hedge – which made a sort of backbone for the whole garden – a rock garden disguised as a dry stream bed.

Some great improvements were forced on me by 'happenstance'; for instance the hedge that I built around the whole garden died. This meant the rock garden was no longer much of a secret surprise, so I stole some more space from the car park and moved boulders and plants to a spot near the dining terrace where, sheltered by a largish *Cercis canadensis* 'Forest Pansy' and a grapefruit tree, it now includes some old stone troughs from Mexico. The plants do well and the

The steps from the rose-covered summer house (once a prosaic carport) ascend through the almost-white garden towards the house at the top of the hill – the first cottage of a three-in-one ownership. White roses, *Hydrangea quercifolia* and a tunnel of foliage embrace you as you climb. *Rubus calycinoides* and *Justicia brande-geeana* 'Chartreuse' cascade down the steps as a stream of green.

stonework makes an entrance to the sitting area and a good foreground for the Matilija poppy that, reclaiming its native ground, has taken over the outside of the driveway. The old space next to the path is being filled in and turned into a mixed border planted with roses and the new alstroemeria hybrids in sherbet colors. This gives me a double border and is much prettier, especially with the evening light behind, but I do still miss the hedge.

The real changes came about ten years ago, when we bought the house next door, and then, a few years later, the one beyond it, ostensibly to gain more living space but really to give me more room to garden. We now have three little cottages in a row, and we live and work in all of them. I fondly imagine they and the outbuildings resemble a little hillside village, and the wide brick path gradually extends to become the main thoroughfare.

The first addition gave me the sunny space for the white garden I had been dreaming of: a paved circle nestled partway down the hill under a *Magnolia grandiflora* and a *Cupressus cashmeriana* now thirty feet tall, grown from a cutting. It's actually the 'mainly white' garden, due to a pink crepe myrtle and a background of white plumbago into which the blue keeps creeping back. Still, I have roses in varying tones of white and every white-flowered thing I can get my hands on.

Below this is my southern California answer to all the nostalgic cowsheds turned garden houses I have seen in England: a summer house made from an abandoned carport. Buried in a giant 'La Mortola' rose, it looks out onto the sundrenched Mediterranean garden, at last a home for all the old roses, giant salvias and silver-leaved plants that languished under the trees. Only someone who has tried to garden in too much shade can know how satisfying this is, and if I can just stop myself from planting too many new trees, maybe I can keep it that way.

The third house, originally buried in blackberry brambles and giant castor bean plants, is now smothered in peach-colored brugmansia and apricot roses. Here are my office and my library, a garden of pink and amber flowers and the last real necessity on my original wish list, the water garden, a plain rectangle in a stone-paved terrace hanging over that view, where we can dream away hours in the warm sun or cool shade drenched in the fragrance of roses and datura and jasmine, watching the circling fish. The sound of water splashing from a grotesque fountain-mask made by my husband is a magical attraction in a dry climate. Dragonflies came immediately and a turtle materialized from somewhere

Some changes were *force majeure* – the hedge planted to surround the whole garden died, so a new double bed now occupies some of that space. With the evening light behind and a view northwards to the mountains opening up beyond, the bed is planted with roses and the new alstroemeria hybrids in sherbet colours. Deceptively, the pink-blossomed tabbebuia is some forty feet away.

on the hillside. The whole pond is now barricaded electrically against the racoons and the blue herons that want to eat my gold and silver koi. It is a kind of *rus in urbe* hazard that doesn't fit most people's idea of life in such a sophisticated city as Los Angeles.

I have come to see that the underlying organization of my random-seeming garden is a series of still points that give purpose to the movement through space and give order and meaning to the wildness of the plantings. I have said that my goal is to have what looks like the remnants of a grand garden in a state of romantic decay. I have probably overshot my mark. We don't usually name our houses and gardens around here, but I've often been tempted to borrow the name of one of the great English estates and call mine Tangley Manor. My whole garden is an experiment; design ideas are sketched out with bits left to finish everywhere, and the planting is a perpetual war between the best way to display plants and the mad greed to have them.

I have also said that this is the end of my wish list, but I lie. My husband sometimes catches me looking the wrong way from one of our vantage points, contemplating an empty hillside next door.

CHRIS ROSMINI, LOS ANGELES, CALIFORNIA

XLVIII

THE THREE AGES OF A PLANTSMAN

'Throughout these distinct phases of my own development and that of the garden, I have always remained true to the natural style of planting . . .'

WHEN IS A GARDEN SECRET? Bredon Springs provides one answer: when few people know it's there and it takes a lot of finding even if they do. The garden lies tucked away behind Ashton church in the little hamlet of Paris. Why Paris? I have some explaining to do.

The name of this assembly of five cottages, grouped in the shape of a Z, dates from the thirteenth century, when they were lived in by the Perys family. With its abundant spring water and deep, rich soil, there was probably a settlement here even earlier, perhaps in prehistoric times. Today the hamlet boasts one Tudor thatched cottage; the others are either eighteenth or nineteenth century with varying degrees of modernization. The two that comprise present-day Bredon Springs were built in 1735 and 1781. The inscription 'WC July 28 1735' is carved above the doorway of the earlier cottage – WC being a Huguenot weaver, one William Cotton.

The one and three-quarter-acre garden of Bredon Springs dates from 1948, when I moved here with my late wife. Over the years my planting policy has changed somewhat, reflecting the evolution of my professional interests, although throughout my main concern has remained the creation of a good home for a variety of plants. At first the botanist in me prevailed and the principal aim was to have the greatest possible number of plant families represented. This developed into an increasing emphasis on the geographical origins of plants, and species from most countries of the world found their way into the garden. Later still the landscape architect took over and I began to see the garden as a canvas in which variety in plant form and texture became more important.

Throughout these distinct phases of my own development and that of the garden, I have always remained true to the natural style of planting and have followed a survival of the fittest philosophy in which the more vigorous plants have often smothered their weaker brethren. Over the years the practice of leaving plants to do as they wish has meant that many choice plants which may have flourished for a time have now disappeared.

The lowering of the water table has taken its own toll. Before the dry years of 1975 and 1976, the central area of the garden was a permanent bog, requiring Wellington boots at all times. Many moisture lovers were established, including candelabra primulas and the fine *Iris kaempferi* 'Oyodo' which I bought from the Slieve Donard nursery in the early 1950s.

The droughts came and the bog went; the surface water has never returned. The deep springs which give their name to the garden are as productive as ever, but the surface soil has become just normally dry, freely

Set in a saucer of land high above the Vale of Evesham, and approached on foot along a track, Bredon Springs is the epitome of a plantsman's secret garden. It was the focus of one man's interests and experiments over nearly half a century, a place where plants and wildlife were given free rein. With Ronald Sidwell's death last year, the special character of his garden, at once a laboratory and natural haven, may also be lost.

drained ground. The impervious clay bed some feet down that formerly kept the surface soil damp probably cracked in the drought and will never again hold water. Visitors to the garden are often puzzled by the vigorous gunneras bursting out of the seemingly dry ground because they do not realize that the huge leaves are in fact fed from the deep spring water many, many feet below the surface through their finger-thick vertical roots.

Most of the garden is high in lime, in some places exceptionally so, but under the top hedge the soil is about neutral and for many years was home to a healthy *Camellia* 'Akashigata' (syn. *C.* 'Lady Clare'). In the south corner of the garden is a bed of tufa at a depth of four feet, and the overlying soil has a free carbonate content of around twenty per cent.

My botanical interests led me to experiment with new and 'improved' forms amongst the mixed plant population of the garden. Always on the lookout for better forms of existing plants, I have bred a number of Bredon specialities. *Lavatera* 'Bredon Springs' is well established and proving a little hardier than most. Its petals have very shallow indentations, in fact they are almost straight-edged, giving the flowers the appearance of pentagonal saucers.

From the purple cultivar 'Marlborough', I raised a batch of clear lavender phlox, which I named 'Grafton' after the next

ABOVE: The house is formed of two eighteenth-century cottages, the earliest built by a Huguenot weaver. Roses and foxgloves emerge from the ground-cover foliage in front of the white-painted door. RIGHT: A border filled with the showy flowers of primulas. Many new varieties of lavatera, phlox, penstemons and wallflower have been raised in this garden, and one of the best aquilegia collections in the country.

hamlet on Bredon Hill. At the time I thought of continuing breeding phlox until I had circumnavigated the hill; alas, I got no further than Grafton. Four penstemons, to which I have given the names of birds – 'Blackbird', 'Raven', 'Osprey' and 'Flamingo' – are now in National Collections. The name 'Bredon Rose' has provisionally been given to a pink pulmonaria with spotted leaves. Judgement day is awaited. The sterile perennial wallflower, *Erysimum* 'Bredon', is among the best of its kind, but possibly the finest of the Bredon Spring plants is the rich purple *Hibiscus syriacus*, which we hope will be on the market before long.

What the garden can now boast is one of the best collections of aquilegias in the country – double and single, spurred and spurless. It started as a simple challenge, to collect all the forms of *Aquilegia vulgaris* described in Parkinson's *Paradisus* and Gerard's *Herball*.

If plants grown naturally are the outstanding contribution to the character of the garden, trees planted since 1948 are beginning to make their mark. When we started, the only trees of consequence, apart from a sapling oak, were fruit trees, mostly dead or dying. A few remain alongside the replacements I have planted over the years – *Ginkgo biloba*, *Taxodium distichum*, *Metasequoia glyptostroboides*, *Magnolia* × *soulangeana*, *M. wilsonii*, *Salix babylonica* var. *pekinensis*

At the top of a simple gravelled flight of stone steps, which merge themselves completely into the background, a perfect natural 'moon gate' leads out of the garden. Day-lilies, geraniums and foxgloves crowd across the slope, spreading out to each side of the path. This is a secret garden of the most unpretentious kind, reflecting the enthusiasm and modesty of its creator.

'Tortuosa', and not least our resident holly, which is a large-leaved form with presumably hermaphrodite flowers and heavy crops of large fruits. A fine specimen golden weeping willow dominates the east corner.

The bird population of Bredon has always been a great joy to me: I regard birds as important as the plants. Sadly their numbers have declined during the last few years. My garden, and those adjoining it, regularly had three nesting pairs of spotted flycatchers. It is now three years since we saw them, and other migrants, notably willow warblers and chiffchaffs, seem similarly to have deserted us.

My approach to gardening has always been to let living things live, whether they are plants, or birds, or insects. No insecticides have been used here for twenty-five years. A few insect 'pests' are tolerated as part of the complex pattern of nature, and we think birds keep the balance right, but I cannot rule out entirely the possibility of having to resort to sprays – how else am I to protect my Solomon's seal from sawfly?

THE LATE RONALD SIDWELL, PARIS, WORCESTERSHIRE

Acknowledgements

The publishers and editors would like to thank the following for their permission to reproduce the photographs in this book:

page 2 Jerry Harpur: p.12-13 Ken Druse: p.14-15 Henry Bowles: p.16 Jerry Harpur: p.17 Henry Bowles: p.18, 19 and 21 Jerry Harpur: p.22 Adam Laipson: p.24 L. Wilbur Zimmerman: p.25-7 Saxon Holt: p.29-33 Marianne Majerus: p.34-5 Neil Campbell-Sharp: p.36, 38 Alexander L. Wallace: p.40-3 Neil Campbell-Sharp: p.44-5 Ken Druse: p.46-51 Jerry Harpur: p.53 Thom Duncan: p.54-5 Southern Press Corps: p.57-8 Condé Nast/Richard Felber: p.58, 60 Larry Albee: p.61-2 Georges Lévêque: p.63-5 Andrew Lawson: p.66-9, 71 Neil Campbell-Sharp: p.72-3 Condé Nast/Richard Felber: p.74-5 Ken Druse: p.76 Johann Mayr: p.77 J. Barry Ferguson: p.80-1 Richard Cheek: p.82-3 Gary Rogers: p.84-6 Camera Press/Gary Rogers: p.88-90 Jerry Harpur: p.92-3 Marijke Heuff: p.94, 95 and 97 Olivier Choppin de Janvry: p.98-102 Marion Nickig: p.105 Camera Press/Gary Rogers: p.106, 108-10 Gary Rogers: p.112, 114 Marion Nickig: p.115 Marijke Heuff: p.116-7 Curtice Taylor: p.118-9, 122-3 Richard Felber: p.124-5 Jerry Harpur: p.126-9 Comtesse d'Andlau: p.130-3 June West: p.134-9 Neil Campbell-Sharp: p.140-3 Jerry Harpur: p.144-7 Andrew Lawson: p.148-9, 151 David McDonald: p.152-5, 157 Andrew Lawson: p.158 Jerry Harpur: p.159 Karen Bussolini: p.160 Barbara Robinson: p.162-3 Andrew Lawson: p.164-7 Cynthia Woodyard: p.168-9 Neil Campbell-Sharp: p.170-3 Marianne Majerus: p.174-7, 179-81 and 183 Jerry Harpur: p.184 Clive Nichols: p.185 Marijke Heuff: p.186 Biofotos Heather Angel: p.187-8 Clive Boursnell; p.189 Neil Campbell-Sharp: p.190, 193 D. C. Young: p.194-7 Cynthia Woodyard: p.198, 200-2 Neil Campbell-Sharp.

The extract on page 10 was taken from 'Hidden Gardens' from *Music for Chameleons* by Truman Capote (HH 1981) © Truman Capote 1975, 1977, 1980 and reproduced by permission of Hamish Hamilton Ltd.

The editors would like to thank William H. Frederick Jr., Steve Lorton, Patrick Taylor, Pat Taylor of the Cottage Garden Society and Wayne Winterrowd for their helpful garden suggestions; Sir Anthony Lambert, Laurence de Bonneval and Gabrielle Sandilands for their skill in translation, Nell Luten Floyd for her assistance with Dan Overly's article, the National Trust for permission to include the garden at Plas-yn-Rhiw, Ulrich Timm for permission to feature gardens from *Schöner Wohnen*, Clive Aslet, editor of *Country Life*, for his informative article on Le Désert de Retz, and Dr Anthony Lord for his assistance with plant names. Above all, we would like to thank Julian Shuckburgh at Ebury Press whose idea it was and who has supported the project throughout, Cindy Richards, our equable, tireless and efficient editor, and all those gardeners whose love for their gardens and sensitivity in writing about them has made this book possible.

The following gardens may be visited but as some are open only periodically, arrangements should be made by contacting the owners at the addresses or telephone numbers given below. Alternatively, details can be found in the following publications: *Gardens of England and Wales* (*), *Gardens of Scotland* (+) and *Historic Houses, Castles and Gardens* (=). See below for publishers' addresses.

Gerda Barlow*
Stancombe Park
Dursley
Gloucestershire G11 6AU

John Casson*
15 Lawrence Street
Chelsea
London SW3 5NE

Olivier Choppin de Janvry
Société Civile de Désert de Retz
6 bis Grande-rue
78290 Croissy sur Seine
France

Robin Compton*=
Newby Hall
Ripon
North Yorkshire HG4 5AE
Tel: 0423 322583

La Comtesse d'Andlau
La Petite Rochelle
22 rue du Prieure
61110 Rémalard
France
(groups only)

Madeleine Dick
The National Trust
Plas-yn-Rhiw
Rhiw
Pwllheli
Gwynedd LL53 8AB

Sonny Garcia, USA
Tel: (0101) 415 584 3512

Laura Fisher
White Meadows Farm,
55 Holly Branch Road
Katonah
New York 10536
USA

Sir Charles and Lady Fraser+
Shepherd House
Inveresk
Midlothian EH21 7TH

Le Duc d'Harcourt
Pavillon de Fantaisie
14220 Thury-Harcourt
(Calvados)
France

Antonio Leidt
Casa de Campo
Cecorico de Basto
Portugal

Hilary Mogford*
Rofford Manor
Little Milton
Oxfordshire OX44 7QQ

Margaret Ogilvie+
House of Pitmuies
Guthrie
By Forfar
Angus DD8 2SN

John Phillips*
Home Covert
Roundway
Devizes
Wiltshire SN10 2JA

Charles L. Reed Jr
Redesdale
Richmond
Virginia 23229-8301

Patricia van Roosmalen
St Pieter 24
3621 Rekem
Belgium

Countess van Lynden van Sandenburg
Walenburg
(c/o The Dutch Garden Society,
tel: 010 31 20 623 5058)

Gardens of England and Wales
The National Gardens Scheme
Hatchlands Park
East Clandon
Guildford
Surrey GU4 7RT
Tel: 0483 211 535

Gardens of Scotland
31 Castle Terrace
Edinburgh EH1 2EL
Tel: 031 229 1870

Historic Houses, Castles and Gardens
Reed Information Services
Windsor Court
East Grinstead House
East Grinstead
West Sussex RH19 1XA
Tel: 0342 326972

INDEX

Page references in *italics* refer to illustrations and captions.

HADDONFIELD PUBLIC LIBRARY

3 7286 00000466 5

712.6
VER   167 370 $40.00

            Verey, Rosemary.
            Secret
            gardens

Haddonfield Public Library
Haddon Ave. and Tanner St.
Haddonfield, NJ 08033

GAYLORD